The Way
to
Eternity

The Way to Eternity

EGYPTIAN MYTH

MYTH AND MANKIND

THE WAY TO ETERNITY: Egyptian Myth
Writers: Fergus Fleming (The Egyptian World, The Divine
Creators, Living with the Gods, The Judgement of Osiris, The
Egyptian Legacy)
Alan Lothian (The Mighty Sons of Re, Tales of Magic and
Fantasy)
Consultant: Dr Joann Fletcher

Created, edited and designed by
Duncan Baird Publishers
Castle House
75–76 Wells Street
London W1P 3RE

DUNCAN BAIRD PUBLISHERS
Managing Editor: Stephen Adamson
Art Director: Gabriella Le Grazie
Editors: Helen Cleary, Ruth Petrie
Designer: Iona McGlashan
Picture Researcher: Anne-Marie Ehrlich
Artworks: Neil Gower, John Woodcock
Map Artworks: Lorraine Harrison
Artwork Borders: Sally Maltby
Editorial Researcher: Simon Ryder
Editorial Assistant: Andrea Buzyn

TIME-LIFE BOOKS
Staff for THE WAY TO ETERNITY: Egyptian Myth
Editorial Manager: Tony Allan
Design Director: Mary Staples
Editorial Production: Jenny Croxall, Justina Cox

Published by Time-Life Books BV, Amsterdam

First Time-Life English language printing 1997

TIME-LIFE is a trademark of
Time Warner Inc, USA

ISBN 0 7054 3503 2

Colour separation by Colourscan, Singapore
Printed and bound by Milanostampa, SpA, Farigliano, Italy

Title page: **King Seti II holding a shrine bearing the head of
the ram god, Amun, *c.*1210BC.**
Contents page: **A wooden statuette of Tutankhamun in
the form of Anubis, the guardian of cemeteries, from the
boy-king's tomb (1323–1333BC).**

30 29 28 27 26 25 24 23 22 21 20 19 18 17 16 15 14 13 12 11 10 9 8 7 6 5 4 3 2

Contents

THE EGYPTIAN WORLD

As they approached the ancient temples of Thebes, the column of French soldiers faltered. One by one they dropped their rifles and stared open-mouthed while their officers shouted orders in vain. The year was 1798 and France had conquered Egypt. Hundreds of miles to the north, on the plateau of Giza, their leader Napoleon Bonaparte gave a more measured response to the three huge pyramids that towered above him. They were crumbling and of various sizes, but even the smallest was magnificent in scale. Napoleon immediately instructed his generals to climb the highest one, and settled down to do some calculations. By the time that the generals had returned, his sums were complete. If all three pyramids were dismantled, he announced, their stones would form a wall three metres high and a third of a metre thick that would surround France.

In the following year, similar discoveries and calculations were made by the French as they swept across the land. Before them lay remnants of a civilization so ancient and yet so advanced that its existence must have been hard for the newcomers to comprehend. The official artist, who had been among the troops at Thebes, was at a loss to represent Egypt's majesty: "Pencil in hand, I passed from object to object, drawn away from one thing by the interest of another ... I felt ashamed of the inadequacy of the drawings I made of such sublime things."

The temples, tombs and monuments that lined the Nile were certainly vestiges of a remarkable society, and the sheer size and longevity of the relics bore fitting tribute to one of the world's most sophisticated civilizations. At its zenith in 1450BC the power of ancient Egypt extended from its border with Libya in the west to the river Euphrates in the east, and from the Nubian deserts in the south to Syria in the north. But its conquests, although impressive, were of secondary importance to Egypt's ruling powers: the heart of the empire lay, as it always had, along the Nile. The riverbanks were a haven in which the Egyptians could nourish their own unique vision of the world.

In due course, the world outside began to encroach upon Egypt. In 343BC the last truly Egyptian ruler was ousted by Persian forces. In the following centuries, the country would be governed by foreigners: Greeks, Romans, Arabs, Turks, French and British. But, despite the overlay of foreign cultures, Egypt's treasures have been preserved and still capture the imagination of the world.

Above: **The pyramids of (from left to right) Menkaure, Khephren and Khufu at Giza, built c.2500BC.**

Opposite: **Mysterious and imposing, the Great Sphinx at Giza has the head of a man and the body of a lion. It dates from c.2500BC, but has been repaired at various times in Egyptian history.**

Ancient Egypt

The main cities, pyramids and religious sites of ancient Egypt are shown with their Egyptian, Greek and modern names.

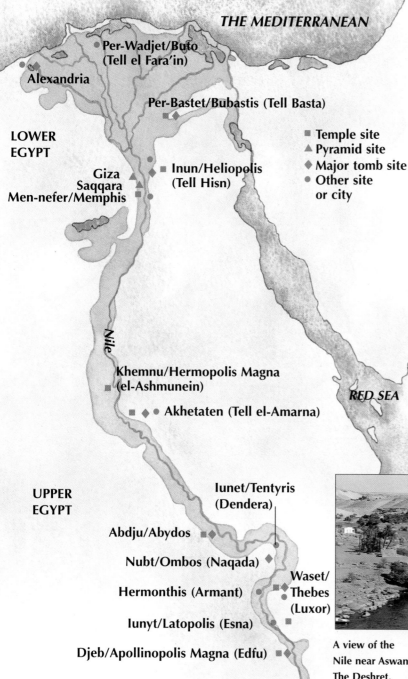

THE MEDITERRANEAN

Per-Wadjet/Buto
(Tell el Fara'in)

Alexandria

Per-Bastet/Bubastis (Tell Basta)

LOWER EGYPT

■ Temple site
▲ Pyramid site
◆ Major tomb site
● Other site or city

Giza
Saqqara
Men-nefer/Memphis

Inun/Heliopolis
(Tell Hisn)

Nile

Khemnu/Hermopolis Magna
(el-Ashmunein)

RED SEA

Akhetaten (Tell el-Amarna)

UPPER EGYPT

Iunet/Tentyris
(Dendera)

Abdju/Abydos

Nubt/Ombos (Naqada)

Hermonthis (Armant)

Waset/
Thebes
(Luxor)

Iunyt/Latopolis (Esna)

Djeb/Apollinopolis Magna (Edfu)

Ombos (Kom Ombo)

Elephantine Island (Aswan)
Philae Island

A view of the Nile near Aswan. The Deshret, "Red Land", is never far from the river, especially around its upper reaches.

Centuries of Civilization

Ancient Egypt was a land of dualities – stark oppositions woven into the very character of the culture. This binary notion was fundamental to Egyptian thought: pre-creation, for example, was known as the time "before there were two things". The primary contrast was that of Deshret versus Kemet – the desert versus the valley and the Delta. Deshret, "The Red Land", was a place of danger, home of marauding nomads and wild animals. Kemet, or "The Black Land", was the fertile land which bordered the Nile, a place where crops flourished and civilized life was possible.

The Nile was vital to the prosperity of Kemet and central to Egypt's economic success. It flowed more than 6700 kilometres from equatorial Africa to the Mediterranean, and was fed at its source by monsoon rains that came in from the Indian Ocean. The rains fell in spring and the flood waters reached Egypt in summer, swamping a one-thousand-kilometre tract of valley floor with water that on receding left behind a rich, black alluvial silt. Between July and October the Nile valley was barely habitable, but when the floods retreated the land was perfect for planting and the resulting harvests were bountiful. By April the Nile had declined to its lowest level and the land began to dry and crack. During the following weeks Egyptians prayed for signs of the next deluge.

However, the flood was not always predictable. Sometimes it was too low, and then people would starve in their thousands – the kind of disaster attributed by one myth to divine retribution for the sins of the world (see page 35). At other times the flood came in such a destructive torrent that whole communities were devastated. Very occasionally it failed to come altogether. Yet, for all their uncertainty, the waters were regarded as a miracle from above – proof that there was an order to the universe and that the Egyptians were its deserving

beneficiaries. It is not surprising that the Greek historian Herodotus, who wrote extensively about Egypt, named the land "The Gift of the Nile".

It is impossible to be sure who were the first people fully to appreciate this gift, but throughout Egypt's history its inhabitants have undoubtedly shown great ingenuity in exploiting the river's potential. Irrigation canals were constructed to divert water to outlying areas, and dykes were built to collect silt to be used as fertilizer on the fields. Cultivation of wheat and barley, the staple crops, was possible almost all year round.

The Nile valley provided a self-contained haven in which Egyptian civilization could thrive. Bounded by deserts to east and west, cataracts (massive rapids) to the south and sea to the north, it was naturally resistant to outside invasion. The river ensured that crops would grow, while also

A detail from a tomb painting in Thebes (1390BC). The dead man is being shown cattle for his inspection, while a scribe holds a papyrus in readiness to record their numbers. There is evidence that cattle-breeding took place along the Nile from a very early date.

providing a conduit for trade. Within this prosperous environment the small farming communities of the initial settlers developed into larger provinces each with its own ruler and its own capital. In time these coalesced into kingdoms.

As befitted the Egyptian concept of duality, the country was originally divided into two distinct kingdoms: Lower Egypt, made up of the flat Delta where the river fanned out and emptied into the Mediterranean, and Upper Egypt, which stretched from the apex of the Delta at Memphis to the

9

Sacred Writing

Writing, for most Egyptians, was a mystery. Less than one per cent of the population was literate – scribes, priests and some of the nobility and royalty. The literate were among the elite and used their script as a medium of power.

Unlike spoken Egyptian which lasted well into the Middle Ages (disappearing only when its last variant, Coptic, was superseded by Arabic), written Egyptian died with the demise of ancient Egypt. The inscriptions on tombs and temples became meaningless without anyone who could read them.

They remained so until 1821, when a French scholar, Jean-François Champollion, inspected a section of inscribed stone detailing the same decree in three scripts – hieroglyphic, demotic (a simplified script used for manuscripts) and Greek. The Rosetta Stone, brought to London by the British army, enabled Champollion to successfully cross-reference the symbols and decipher their meanings.

Initially, written Egyptian took the form of ideograms – pictorial representations of an object or an idea. Sprawled decoratively across temples and tombs, hieroglyphs, or "sacred words", as the Greeks called them, were finely executed and apparently very simple – a picture of an owl meant "owl". But with time the language grew more complex. Some hieroglyphs came to assume phonetic values; known as phonograms, they represented individual consonants or combinations of consonants – the owl could also be the equivalent of an English "m", the symbol for a house also represented the sound "pr" and a bee could stand for a syllable or translate as "bit".

Hieroglyphs were mutable. The ideogram depicting a razor, for example, changed shape over the centuries to match the types of razor in current use. Hieroglyphic script could be read from left to right, right to left, top to bottom or, sometimes, from the middle out. The symbols pointed the way. If an ideogram with a face, say a bird, faced left, then you read the script from left to right; if it faced right, you read from right to left.

A detail from the Abydos King List, noting previous monarchs worthy of receiving gifts from Rameses II, *c.*1290BC. Hieroglyphs ("sacred words") were only used for sacred texts.

The system of hieroglyphs was reserved largely for ceremony, and by 2600BC an easier script, hieratic, had emerged for everyday use. Hieratic was a more fluid version of hieroglyphic which enabled scribes to present a legible account without having to resort to the complicated formalities of hieroglyphs. Demotic, known to the Egyptians as *sekh shat* ("writing for documents"), then replaced hieratic in the sixth century BC, and might in time have evolved into a national script, had the last dynasties been less rigid in their outlook.

cataracts at Aswan in the south. Around 3100BC these two areas were united under one ruler who wore both the Red crown of Lower Egypt and the White crown of Upper Egypt. During the New Kingdom (*c*.1539–1075BC), the Egyptian king came to be described as *per-aa*, "great house", originally

the Nile or the animals that lived around it. As the settlements grew into provinces (or "nomes" as they were called in the Ptolemaic period), the deity worshipped in the capital of each region gained prominence. The two kingdoms that emerged and were eventually unified were symbolized by two

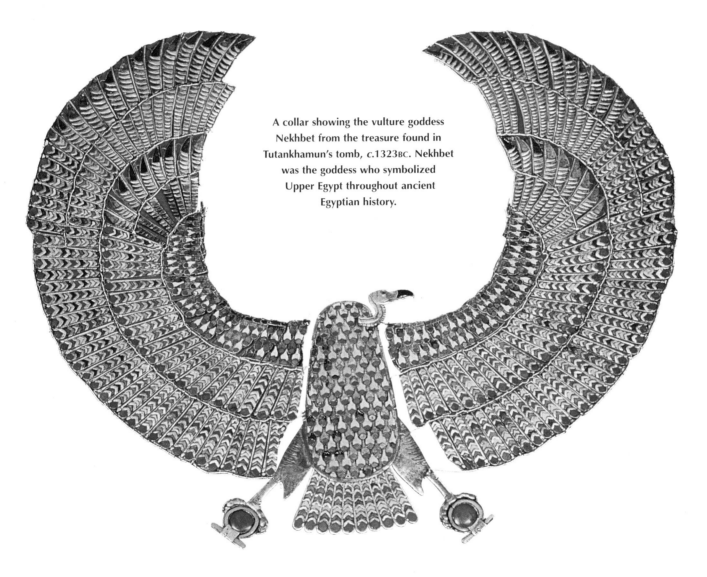

A collar showing the vulture goddess Nekhbet from the treasure found in Tutankhamun's tomb, *c*.1323BC. Nekhbet was the goddess who symbolized Upper Egypt throughout ancient Egyptian history.

a reference to the monarch's residence. Our use of the title "pharaoh" comes from the Greek corruption of this Egyptian term.

Politically Egypt moved towards unity, but the situation with regard to religion was altogether more complex. Early Egyptians were ancestor worshippers, but as they formed settlements, so local deities emerged. These deities usually represented

goddesses. The northern kingdom was represented by Wadjet, the cobra goddess of Lower Egypt, while Nekhbet, the vulture goddess of Upper Egypt, prevailed in the south.

The Egyptians who adopted these new gods did not abandon the old ones, but merely expanded their devotion to accommodate them. While acknowledging Wadjet, inhabitants of a

11

Lower Egyptian settlement might also worship a variety of deities – their forebears, their own local god, and any number of "universal" gods, representing elemental forces.

Beliefs travelled and intermingled. In 450BC Herodotus noticed that the priesthood of Thebes, in Upper Egypt, venerated a pet crocodile. The crocodile represented the god Sobek, whose centre of worship lay to the north in the aptly named town of Crocodilopolis. The Thebans were clearly worshipping another district's god, although Thebes was the cult centre of Amun-Re, the highest deity for much of Egypt's history.

The first pharaohs must have realized that

their status was precarious. To reaffirm their power the concept of the god-king was born. Each pharaoh came to be considered as the earthly embodiment of the god Horus – the son of Osiris and Isis – who was the image of both royal and celestial power. When the pharaoh died he joined the gods. The dual role ascribed to the pharaoh was consistent with the Egyptians' tendency to fuse together different ideas and beliefs, which they did extensively in their religion. By about 2800BC the principle of the god-king had been accepted as the ideological basis on which every pharaoh should rule. As one inscription put it, the pharaoh was "superintendent of all things which heaven dispenses and the earth produces".

The religious aspect of the pharaoh's role, however, was to a large extent delegated to his high priests, who acted as intermediaries between

This 11th-century BC papyrus from *The Book of the Dead* shows two representations of the eye of Horus. Generally shown as a falcon, Horus was a powerful sky god who embodied kingship.

An illustration of dancing girls, after a tomb painting from the 18th Dynasty (1550–1307BC). The many scenes of dancing indicate that it was a common feature of festivals and celebrations, and also of ordinary entertainment.

heaven and earth. As monarch, however, he had to run a large and increasingly sophisticated realm, and his political obligations were vast. Day-to-day administration was delegated to a ministry of nobles, bureaucrats and priests. At the helm was the vizier, who was accountable, with lesser officials, for the administration of justice, the controlling of trade and foreign tribute, and the assessment and gathering of taxes.

Tax assessment possibly involved the use of Nilometers. These devices consisted of steps against which the height of the Nile was measured. As the flood determined the year's crop and hence a farmer's yield, scholars have suggested that the water level served to set the size of contributions.

On the whole, Egypt's political system ran smoothly, although, inevitably, there were periods of turbulence. Dynasties rose and fell as regional nobles seized the throne, or foreign powers invaded. Occasionally a pharaoh's misrule brought chaos to the country. But after each upheaval the system reasserted itself, the new monarch assuming, like his predecessors, the mantle of Horus. After a brief period of turmoil, Egyptian life returned to its previous harmony, punctuated by the annual flood.

The Two Lands

Agriculture was the major source of Egypt's income, and most of the population worked the fields. All those who did so were liable to see a percentage of their produce being taken as tax by the vizier's men. During the months when the Nile was in flood, the general population might also be expected to labour on a number of royal projects such as the building of a pyramid. But the Nile's bounty was so great that even after the taxes had been collected, people could live what was for the time a relatively comfortable life.

Building huge stone monuments may have been gruelling, but the labourers seem to have been comparatively well treated, receiving adequate provisions and facilities. Accounts of the lives of the royal craftsmen make it clear that they had one day off in ten. There were also official holidays, such as the New Year and the harvest festival, which could last for several days. Cardinal family events such as births and deaths were occasions for private ceremony. The walls of Egyptian tombs bear numerous depictions of the dancing and feasting that accompanied such celebrations.

The elite – the aristocracy, the high priests and the higher-ranking bureaucrats – enjoyed a

13

standard of living that was well beyond the reach of the labouring classes. Many possessed luxurious town houses of two or three stories in which they were surrounded by servants. They also owned villas in the countryside, where they escaped to enjoy the life of prosperous landowners. There they and their wives enjoyed leisure and wealth, with money to spend on their appearance. For example, eyepaints made from green malachite (copper ore) and black galena (lead ore), were worn by men, women and children alike. They were believed to have medicinal qualities, and also acted as an insect repellent, as well as offering protection against the glare of the sun's rays.

The nobleman pursuing wildfowl in this wall painting of *c.*1390BC would have been hunting for sport.

Egyptian society, like any other, was one of contrast and division, but it was not completely inequitable. Women in ancient Egypt had greater freedom than elsewhere in the ancient world – they could draw up wills, buy and sell property, and even run their own businesses. Similarly, not only higher-class citizens but even field workers were given legal rights in a complex and inclusive system of law. And, whatever their status in Egyptian society, everybody could look forward to the possibility of an afterlife. By the time of the New Kingdom at least, eternity was no longer held to be exclusively reserved for the upper classes.

TIME LINE Ancient Egyptian History	EARLY DYNASTIC PERIOD 2920–2575BC	OLD KINGDOM 2575–2134BC	FIRST INTERMEDIATE PERIOD 2134–2040BC	MIDDLE KINGDOM 2040–1640BC

There is no consensus over the exact dating of events before 664BC, and most of the dates given here before that year represent approximations generally agreed upon by Egyptologists. Only the names of better-known pharaohs have been included, under the dynasty when they ruled.

First Dynasty
2920–2770BC
Second Dynasty
2770–2649BC
Third Dynasty
2649–2575BC
Djoser

The first pyramid was built by King Djoser in the 3rd Dynasty and was stepped.

The Great Sphinx at Giza dates from the 4th Dynasty.

Fourth Dynasty
2575–2465BC
Snofru, Khufu, Khephren, Menkaure
Fifth Dynasty
2465–2323BC
Sixth Dynasty
2323–2150BC
Teti, Pepi II
Seventh and Eighth Dynasties 2150–2134BC

Ninth and Tenth Dynasties
2134–2040BC
Eleventh Dynasty
(before reunification of Egypt) 2134–2040BC

A typical tomb painting.

In this era Osiris's influence extended beyond royalty.

Eleventh Dynasty (after unification) 2040–1991BC
Montuhotep Nebhepetre
Twelfth Dynasty
1991–1783BC
Thirteenth Dynasty
1783–1640BC
Fourteenth Dynasty
(ruled concurrently with the 13th & 15th Dynasties)

The Afterlife

The idea of death as only a temporary interruption of life probably goes back far into Egyptian prehistory – it was suggested naturally by the annual rebirth of vegetation after the Nile flood. The identification of the deceased with the god Osiris, who was murdered by his brother Seth and brought back to life by his wife Isis (see pages 76–77), added a new element, which came to play a crucial role in royal and private funerary rituals.

However confident or otherwise they felt of survival beyond the grave, the Egyptians were certainly obsessed with mortality, and even on the liveliest occasions they chose to remind themselves of death. Herodotus reported: "When the wealthy give a party and the banquet is finished, a man carries round among the guests a wooden image of a corpse in a coffin, carved and painted to resemble the real thing as closely as possible. He shows it to each guest in turn, and says, 'Look on this body, as you drink and make merry, since you will be just like it when you are dead.'" The story underlines the Egyptians' ready acceptance of the reality of death. Egyptian religion was based essentially on what people could see or touch – animals, the sun, the moon, the Nile and the harvest – and this acute sense of the physical extended to what was thought to happen to the spirit in the afterlife. It was vital that the body remain intact to provide shelter for the individual's soul after death. And so everyone took pains to ensure that their bodies were preserved as adequately as possible.

In death, as in life, Egypt was dependent upon its topography: whereas Kemet's black earth sustained the living, Deshret's red sands conserved the dead. The desert's dryness was a natural preservative, and everybody, pharaoh and peasant alike, was buried there. The poorest made do with a shallow grave in the sand, but the body of a pharaoh required special treatment. He had to be effectively preserved in a manner appropriate to his status as a god-king. This need led to great innovations in design and building techniques. Initially, pharaonic tombs were square, mud-brick edifices built in the sand, surrounded by pits packed with all the things that the ruler might need in the afterlife, such as food, weapons and

SECOND INTERMEDIATE PERIOD 1640–1550BC	**NEW KINGDOM** 1550–1070BC	**THIRD INTERMEDIATE PERIOD** 1070–712BC	**LATE PERIOD** 712–332BC	**GRAECO-ROMAN PERIOD** 332BC–AD395

Tutankhamun's mask.

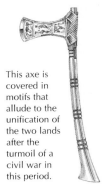

Fifteenth, Sixteenth and Seventeenth Dynasties (in a divided country all ruled concurrently with each other) Seqenenre, Kamose

This axe is covered in motifs that allude to the unification of the two lands after the turmoil of a civil war in this period.

Eighteenth Dynasty 1550–1307BC Hatshepsut, Tuthmosis III, Amenhotep III, Akhenaten, Tutankhamun (see above) **Nineteenth Dynasty** 1307–1196BC Seti I, Rameses II **Twentieth Dynasty** 1196–1070BC Rameses III

Twenty-First Dynasty 1070–945BC **Twenty-Second Dynasty** 945–712BC Sheshonq I **Twenty-Third Dynasty** 828–712BC **Twenty-Fourth Dynasty** 724–712BC **Twenty-Fifth Dynasty** 770–712BC

A vase, typical of household objects of this time.

Twenty-Fifth Dynasty 712–664BC **Twenty-Sixth Dynasty** 664–525BC **Twenty-Seventh Dynasty (First Persian)** 525–404BC **Twenty-Eighth Dynasty** 404–399BC **Twenty-Ninth Dynasty** 399–380BC **Thirtieth Dynasty** 380–343BC Second Persian 343–332BC

Macedonian Kings 332–304BC Alexander the Great **Ptolemaic Dynasty** 304–30BC Cleopatra VII **Roman Emperors** 30BC–AD395

Left, above: An amulet of Shu, god of air, who gained popularity in the 26th Dynasty. *Above*: A Graeco-Roman tomb.

furniture. In the earliest years of Egyptian history, servants were considered essential even in the afterlife, and were sacrificed so as to accompany their master on the journey to the underworld. For the benefit of one early pharaoh, Djer, who ruled around 2900BC, several hundred members of his retinue appear to have been killed so that they might serve him after death. But the practice of human sacrifice was short-lived: eventually, bodies were replaced by effigies.

The custom of including other paraphernalia in the tomb was also rationalized in later years. As well as stores of food, an individual might be given a scythe in order to harvest his or her own crop. Similarly, wall paintings and carvings were used as substitutes for real offerings, which could not be made indefinitely.

This drive towards moderation, however, was not applied to the tombs themselves. From the early days of the Old Kingdom, they grew steadily in size and magnificence. The early mud-bricked structures were in time placed in tiers to form a stepped pyramid. The bricks themselves were replaced with more enduring material in the form of local limestone. A limited amount of granite was used for lining some of the pyramids' interior chambers and for facing some of the exterior masonry. The stepped shape – such as that of the Saqqara Pyramid (see page 30) – later gave way to the smooth sides of the true pyramid.

The tomb-building process became lengthier as hundreds of workers were mobilized to transport the stone, cut it to shape and assemble it according to an architect's instructions. In some cases the logistical and engineering skills involved seem almost incredible today. The Great Pyramid at Giza, for example, commissioned in about 2550BC by the pharaoh Khufu, stood 230 metres square at its base and reached a height of 146

After mummification the body was usually placed in a coffin (or even two or three, one inside the other) constructed in human form and often elaborately painted with mythological scenes. This mummy case from Thebes, c.1050BC, was made for an anonymous singer.

16

metres. It comprised 2,300,000 blocks of stone averaging 2.5 tonnes in weight, although the heaviest reached 15 tonnes. The construction continued through most of Khufu's twenty-three-year reign. It took many thousands of men to build not only the pyramid but also the inclined ramps necessary to haul blocks to the upper courses.

In time pyramid-building went out of fashion, and burial chambers became popular instead. However, tombs entailed a drawback that burial in the Deshret never had: isolated by masonry from the desiccating sand, bodies began to decay. This was unthinkable, and the problem had to be solved if the physical integrity of the dead was to be preserved. The Egyptians looked for alternative ways of maintaining the body in pristine form so that it was fully prepared for the its journey to the afterlife. Embalming was the answer (see pages 96–99).

The earliest embalming technique was to wrap the corpse in resin-impregnated linen, a process now known as mummification (a term which derives from the Persian-Arabic word *moumiya*, meaning "bitumen" or "pitch"). As the embalmers became more proficient, mummification became longer and more complex. The results were impressive: mummified remains have been found that are possibly five thousand years old.

It was not only the body that had to be preserved and commemorated. The Egyptians set great store by naming people and objects, and the name itself was seen as a living entity. Accordingly, ceremonies for the dead continued in temples and homes even after the corpse had been preserved, with the deceased's name being honoured in daily prayers. The spirit was also nourished every day with offerings of food and sustenance.

A state-funded priesthood, established to administer to the religious needs of the royal dead, had the particular responsibility of immortalizing successive generations of pharaohs and their wives. Many priests held their office by inheritance, as a result of belonging to families to which the same job was guaranteed from one generation to the next.

By the end of the Middle Kingdom, pyramid-building had died out, and instead pharaohs had secret rock-cut tombs built for them with separate mortuary temples some distance away. This site at Deir el-Bahri contains two royal mortuary temples, the larger being that of Queen Hatshepsut (1473–1458BC).

The pharaoh's example was followed by many of his subjects, although on a lesser scale. Nobles and courtiers in the Old Kingdom had their own tombs, usually clustered around that of their ruler. Their bodies, like those of the pharaohs, were embalmed, and their names also were commemorated by priests to whom they left substantial endowments. (When the endowments ran out, commemoration continued through the religious texts inscribed in the tomb.) Even minor officials contrived some form of constructed burial place, albeit sometimes only a modest rock-cut tomb in a cliff along the Nile.

The Last Dynasties

For much of its history Egypt was governed from the city of Memphis, strategically situated at the point where Upper Egypt met Lower Egypt. Some twenty kilometres to the northwest, on the plateau of Giza, was the group of pyramids that would so impress Napoleon and his soldiers, as well as millions of later visitors. Giza was one of the major burial sites for pharaohs. But there were many others littered up and down the Nile, and among the most spectacular was the cluster of tombs and temples at Thebes.

During the First Intermediate Period, Thebes assumed a prominent role, eventually becoming the administrative centre for Upper Egypt. It was also a major religious site and for more than a millennium Egyptian rulers were buried and worshipped there. Visitors of the time must have been awed – just as Napoleon's soldiers would later be – by the city's grandeur. On the west bank of the Nile stood rows of mortuary temples, serving the royal burial grounds hidden in the desert cliffs beyond. On the east bank lay Karnak, an astonishing ninety-eight-hectare complex of temples, statues, obelisks, pylons (ceremonial gateways) and courtyards dedicated to the sun god Amun-Re. From Karnak an avenue of stone sphinxes (human-headed lions that were symbols of royal power) led southwest to the smaller yet still impressive complex at Luxor, constructed by Amenhotep III in honour of Amun-Kamutef.

Wherever the seat of power lay, Thebes was the touchstone by which all other places were judged. It was widely held to be the most splendid city of all. As one scribe declared:

"What do they say every day in their hearts,
those who are far from Thebes?
They spend their day blinking at its name,
if only we had it, they say –
The bread there is tastier than cakes made
with goose fat,
its water is sweeter than honey,
one drinks of it till one gets drunk.
O! That is how one lives at Thebes."

Thebes was a thoroughly "Egyptian" city. Throughout history, it was the cultural bastion of Egypt. Whenever invaders entered the country, they usually established themselves in the Delta only to have to confront armies from Thebes, far to the south, marching north to repulse them. If the intruders could not be driven out and assumed nationwide control, Thebes still acted as a repository for the culture that eventually reasserted itself. But as the invasions became more frequent and the aggressors more powerful, so Thebes's cultural influence diminished.

By the middle of the first millennium BC, Egypt's power was on the wane. Weakened by internecine struggles, its borders began to crumble. In 525BC it became part of the Persian Empire, and although it regained its independence in the following century, in 343BC the Persians returned, defeating and killing Nectanebo II, the last truly Egyptian pharaoh. Following his death his tomb was violated and his sarcophagus later taken to Alexandria to be used as a public bath.

Barely a decade later, the Persians themselves fled before Alexander the Great. Thereafter, Egypt was ruled for three hundred years by his successors, the Greek-speaking Ptolemies. The last of these was Cleopatra; after she committed suicide in 30BC, Egypt became a province of the Roman Empire. The *coup de grâce* occurred in the fourth century AD, when Christianity became the Empire's religion. The Emperor Theodosius I ordered the closure of the temples, and the last living vestiges of Egypt's native religion were swept away.

The civilization of ancient Egypt then vanished with astonishing rapidity. Within a year, sand had drifted into spaces that had been hallowed for millennia. In the following centuries, tombs, which even during Egypt's zenith had been prey to tomb-robbers, were ransacked with a new ruthlessness. Pyramids were treated with indifference, and were partially dismantled to provide stone for building purposes. The final indignity came when enterprising merchants discovered a new medicine that they claimed could cure any illness. Its main ingredient was powdered mummy.

Both Rameses II (1290–1224BC), who built this gateway or pylon, and
Alexander the Great (332–323BC) regarded the temple of Amun-Khamutef
at Luxor (initially built by Amenhotep III) as sufficiently important to
merit additions. Luxor is one of three main religious sites at Thebes.

SYMBOLS AND AMULETS

A mulets manifest both the intricate workmanship of Egyptian craftsmen and the complexities of religious symbolism in Egypt. First made in the Predynastic period (as early as 4000BC), amuletic jewellery was considered essential both to earthly security and to the well-being of the deceased's spirit in the afterlife. An amulet was worn as an ornament but its primary purpose was to protect or bestow magical benefits upon the wearer. Although they were made from every sort of material, amulets were most commonly given a bright faience glaze. Gods or goddesses (or their animal manifestations), sacred animals and human figures are the most frequent themes.

This necklace found in Tutankhamun's tomb (he died in 1323BC) features one of the most powerful protective amulets – the *wedjat* (or Eye of Horus; see page 57), which symbolized wholeness. The smaller element takes the form of the two *djed* pillars that represent stability flanking the *sa* amulet of protection.

Above: The ibis amulet representing Thoth, god of knowledge, had a funerary function, as did the gold jackal. The squatting figure of Amun-Re, however, would have been worn by the living.

Above: This glazed earthenware amulet of Taweret, the fertility goddess, who took the form of a hippopotamus, was probably worn by a woman in the belief that it would protect her during childbirth.

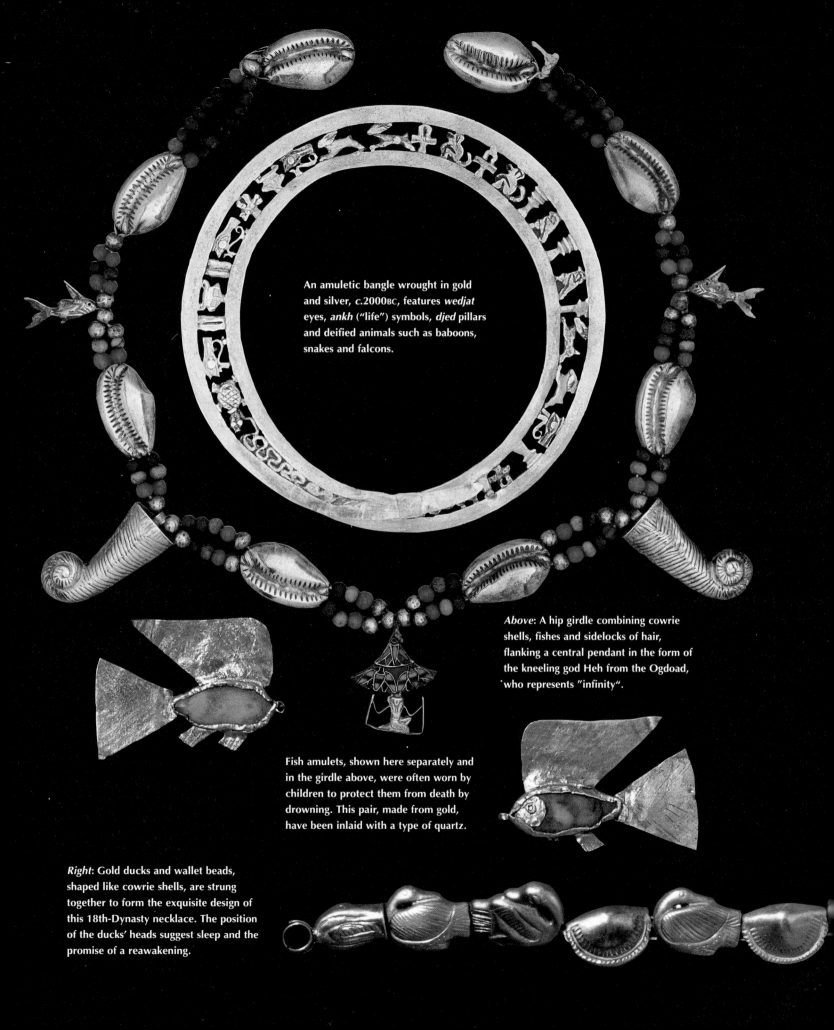

An amuletic bangle wrought in gold
and silver, c.2000BC, features *wedjat*
eyes, *ankh* ("life") symbols, *djed* pillars
and deified animals such as baboons,
snakes and falcons.

Above: A hip girdle combining cowrie
shells, fishes and sidelocks of hair,
flanking a central pendant in the form of
the kneeling god Heh from the Ogdoad,
who represents "infinity".

Fish amulets, shown here separately and
in the girdle above, were often worn by
children to protect them from death by
drowning. This pair, made from gold,
have been inlaid with a type of quartz.

Right: Gold ducks and wallet beads,
shaped like cowrie shells, are strung
together to form the exquisite design of
this 18th-Dynasty necklace. The position
of the ducks' heads suggest sleep and the
promise of a reawakening.

THE DIVINE CREATORS

In 712BC a new pharaoh, Shabaka, ascended the throne by conquest rather than inheritance. Although he was an outsider, he respected the system that he had seized and was shocked to discover, while on a tour of Memphis, that a sacred papyrus scroll narrating a creation myth was being eaten by worms. Shabaka immediately instructed that its remaining contents be inscribed on a slab of basalt, to preserve its message.

The Shabaka Stone survived, but not in the way that the pharaoh had envisaged. By the time that modern archaeologists discovered the slab, it had been transformed into a millstone. The alteration had damaged the inscription, yet the resulting image was curiously apt. A hole for the mill shaft had been drilled through the centre of the slab, and channels (necessary for the grinding of corn) radiated from this hole. An inscription describing the creation of the world had thereby been incised with markings that happened to form a symbol of the sun, considered by the Egyptians to be the primary source of life.

To express their appreciation of its all-important power, the Egyptians worshipped the sun in the form of various gods. These were uppermost in Egypt's pantheon, the supreme solar deity being Re of Heliopolis. Re existed from the beginning of time; he was also a creator deity, but only in conjunction with his other god forms, Atum and Khepri.

There were three principal creation myths, found in different cults that flourished in the three major cities: Hermopolis Magna, Heliopolis and Memphis. The details of these myths were expressed in Egyptian iconography, hieroglyphs and ritual, but it is only from later Greek and Roman sources that more complete narrative accounts have survived. Our perception of the early creation stories, therefore, depends partly upon our understanding of pictorial representations. For all the differences between them, fundamental ingredients in all these views of the world's origins were the sources of life that the Egyptians saw about them – the Nile waters and the sun.

Left: **The Theban king of the gods, Amun-Re, depicted in a large state document of Rameses III (20th Dynasty).**

Opposite: **Re, the sun god, was frequently depicted as a falcon, wearing the solar disc headdress. He symbolized an essential source of creation – the sun. From a version of *The Book of the Dead*, c.1150BC.**

Order out of Chaos

The Egyptians' understanding of the universe was limited by what they could see around them. According to ancient texts, the waters of chaos (thought to be devoid of life) surrounded their world, which was separated into three parts: the earth, the sky, and the underworld (which was known as the *Duat).* The sun journeyed into the perilous *Duat* at night, which was why it could not be seen. This lucid but somewhat disturbing vision raised one crucial question: how had life been formed in the first place?

In their accounts of the mysteries of creation the Egyptians were inspired by the natural world. They observed the changing levels of the Nile and the alluvial silt that was left behind as the annual flood receded. The silt was rich in nutrients that enabled crops to flourish. Each year the newly fertilized earth formed mounds of land that were seen for the first time as the waters retreated. The Egyptians based their view of the waters of chaos on the Nile, surmising that they too held a procreative energy. And so they concluded that creation had started with a similar mound that rose above the primeval waters.

The mound was central to all Egyptian creation myths, and its existence was never disputed. The god Tatjenen, whose name translates as "Risen Land", personified this primordial feature. But the precise origins of the mound provoked debate: where had it first arisen? Every major religious centre claimed that it had emerged at its own site, and theologians spent a great deal of time debating which deity had first appeared there.

The creation myths themselves varied from place to place. At Heliopolis, in Lower Egypt, a family of nine original gods, the Ennead (or "Group of Nine"), as the Greeks later called them, was worshipped. The first god to materialize on the mound was Atum, Lord of Heliopolis, described as "he who came into being of himself". He immediately started to produce more gods: according to one part of the *Pyramid Texts*, he "took his penis in his hand and ejaculated through it to produce the twins Shu (Air) and Tefnut (Moisture)," while elsewhere in these texts Atum is said to have "spluttered out Shu and spat up Tefnut". Thus the world's atmosphere was formed. Shu and Tefnut then coupled to produce Geb (Earth) and Nut (Sky). Nut and Geb begat four children: Osiris and Seth, the opposing gods of order and disorder, and their consorts Isis and Nephthys. From these origins all other life came into being.

A statuette of Ptah, held to be the creator of the world by the people of Memphis, who believed that he brought everything into being by thought and word alone.

The Birth of the Year

Originally, the year had only 360 days. This changed when Atum discovered an illicit passion between his two grandchildren, Nut (earth) and Geb (sky), whose union deprived the world of its atmosphere.

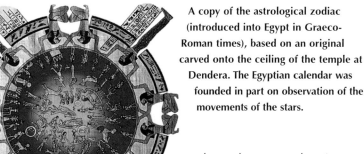

A copy of the astrological zodiac (introduced into Egypt in Graeco-Roman times), based on an original carved onto the ceiling of the temple at Dendera. The Egyptian calendar was founded in part on observation of the movements of the stars.

According to a Greek version of this tale, Nut and Geb were so closely intertwined that there was no room for anything between them. This angered Atum, who ordered their father Shu, god of air, to separate them. Shu did so by standing on Geb and hoisting Nut above his head so that they could not touch each other. Nut, however, was already pregnant. In his wrath Atum cursed her: she was allowed to give birth, he announced, but she was forbidden to do so on any of the 360 days that made up the year at that time. Among the gods whom Atum created was Thoth, god of wisdom. Thoth loved Nut and decided to help her by challenging the other gods to a game of draughts in which he gambled for more time. He won five days, and by adding them to the existing year he created time for Nut to give birth on successive days to her five children: Osiris, Horus, Seth, Isis and Nephthys. Thoth's wisdom and cunning had gained Egypt a full calendar year.

Ptah, the Creator God

The Heliopolitan doctrine was markedly physical in character. Atum's act was seen as procreative even though he had no partner: the theologians ascribed female qualities to his hand, which eventually gained the status of a goddess. In Memphis, however, the creator god Ptah's act of creation was contemplative rather than physically active. Ptah was part of a triad of deities, along with his consort the lioness-goddess Sekhmet and the lotus god Nefertem, understood to be Ptah's son. Like the god Khnum (see pages 30–32), Ptah was a patron of craftsmen, and his high priest was called "greatest of the controllers of craftsmen". Ptah created by intellectual effort alone, thinking things into existence with the ideas that emanated from his heart and the names that then issued from his tongue. For the Egyptians, the heart was the seat of intellect and the source of any thought, which the tongue then spoke to make real. By uttering a litany of names Ptah was able to produce the gods and all of Egypt, including the cities, shrines, temples and nomes.

The Memphite creation myth exalting Ptah did not supersede the myth of Atum as creator, nor did it reject Atum's actions on the mound. The two myths coexisted: Atum's material presence was symbolized by the sacred hill at every religious site, while Ptah's intellectual presence was in "all gods, all people, all cattle, all creeping things that live". Some variations included both Ptah and Atum: the Ennead and Atum were thought of as the lips and teeth of Ptah. In another fusion, with the god Tatjenen who personified the primeval mound, Ptah was linked to the sacred hill.

Ptah was one of the oldest creator gods and there were temples to him all over Egypt, but he did not rise to ultimate supremacy in the

Sources of Egyptian Myth

The myths of the Egyptians were referred to by various classical writers including the Greek historian Herodotus, who visited the country in 450BC. However, most of our knowledge comes from the discovery of abundant sacred texts and images protected by the desert sand across Egypt.

This section of *The Book of the Dead* shows eight discs, representing the four gods and goddesses of the Ogdoad. They emerged as the basic elements from the primeval chaos. The god Nun is also shown here, holding up the sun barque above the primordial waters.

The main source for ancient Egyptian myths concerning creation, the gods and rebirth are tombs, coffins and scrolls. However the principal purpose of the texts and images recorded there was not to recount the myths but to assist the dead on their perilous journey into the afterlife. The stories are therefore only implicit. Further insight into the Egyptians' beliefs is given by inscriptions on temple walls, spells, prayers, incantations and hymns.

Some of the most striking accounts of the unfolding of creation have survived on the interior and exterior surfaces of wooden coffins. Information about Atum's "divine masturbation" (see page 24) was included among the *Coffin Texts* (as they are known) found at Bersha, near Hermopolis. They were made for those who could afford an elaborate burial.

The earliest funerary texts, known as the *Pyramid Texts*, date from the early third millennium BC. They were carved onto the walls of nine royal pyramids of the Old Kingdom and were composed exclusively for the king. However, by the New Kingdom such texts had evolved, via the *Coffin Texts*, into the so-called *Book of the Dead*, which was reproduced individually for the deceased. Known to Egyptians as "The Chapters of Coming Forth By Day", these widely available texts were written on papyrus and could contain up to two hundred different chapters, according to the wealth of the owner. The papyrus was rolled up and placed in a special container in the coffin alongside the corpse. (One copy, dating from the fourth century BC, follows a theme found in earlier *Coffin Texts* in its reference to Atum, the original "All".)

In the hearts of all Egyptians was the fear that they might fail to speak the correct words that would help them reach eternity when their heart was weighed against the feather of truth before the throne of Osiris, Lord of the underworld. A typical formula from the *Book of the Dead*, offering defensive spells for the judgement scene, proclaims: "Oh Far Strider, who came forth from Heliopolis, I have done no falsehood; Oh Fire-embracer who came forth from Kheraha, I have not robbed."

Temple libraries were repositories for a whole range of texts, but until the Ptolemaic period few were of a non-funerary nature.

pantheon. By the Late Period he had combined with other gods, to become Ptah-Sokar-Osiris, a god of the dead. When the Greeks arrived in Egypt, they identified Ptah with their smith god Hephaistos, and one of Ptah's shrines in Memphis, called *Hwt-ka-Ptah* ("Mansion of the Spirit of Ptah"), came to refer to the whole region: its Greek form *Aeguptos* gave us the modern name, "Egypt".

The Ogdoad and Amun

In Hermopolis, further to the south in the centre of Egypt, local myth dealt as much with what had occurred before the mound was formed as with what had happened after. The Hermopolitan Ogdoad, or "Group of Eight", consisted of four pairs of male and female deities who inhabited the primeval waters before the world existed. The males took the form of frogs and the females were represented as snakes, although sometimes they were alternatively depicted as baboons.

The gods and goddesses were paired to represent four different aspects of the universe before the world was created: Nun and his consort Naunet together personified the original formless ocean, Heh and Hauhet symbolized infinity, Kek and Kauket embodied darkness, and Amun and Amaunet were the dual incarnation of hidden power. The divinities signified all that could not be seen or touched – they comprised the antithesis of life. Yet, as male and female pairs, they represented at the same time the *possibility* of life. They were also linked with the sun by their association with baboons, who greeted the dawn with howls.

Initially the Ogdoad was divided into two groups, male and female; but, at a certain point in their existence, the two sexes were driven together. Although the exact details of this cataclysmic meeting are unknown, the myths from Hermopolis describes the event as having come about at the command of Thoth, the patron deity of the city. No doubt the claim was intended to promote his status.

This relief depicts three baboons associated with the god of knowledge, Thoth. The animals were also celebrated by those who worshipped the sun god because they appeared to greet the dawn with a chorus of howls.

The violent meeting between the two groups produced a tremendous upheaval, which in turn engendered the primordial mound. The mound itself contained a cosmic egg, which hatched to reveal the young sun god. As the shell fell apart, the mound turned into an "Island of Flame", and the new-born sun god ascended the sky to his rightful position in the heavens. This event was considered in Hermopolis to be the very first sunrise to take place in Egypt. The Ogdoad had thus become "the fathers and mothers who came into being at the start, who gave birth to the sun and who created Atum".

The Hermopolitan concept, which likened the birth of the universe to a cataclysm, in some ways anticipates modern "Big Bang" theories. It is tempting to speculate that the Egyptians, who were accomplished astronomers, based this concept on their observations of the night sky. It is more likely, though, that the idea represented an especially intense example of their view that life was made up of binary opposites. In a clash of cosmic genders the basis for life was laid down.

The Theban view of creation was different again. In Thebes Amun was all-powerful, whereas in Hermopolis he was just one of a number of

The Wandering Eye

On his crown the pharaoh bore the protective uraeus, the cobra that symbolized Wadjet, goddess of Lower Egypt. Wadjet was said to protect the king by spitting fire at his enemies. In the creation myth of Heliopolis we learn why the uraeus was so powerful.

Atum created his children Shu and Tefnut (see page 24) to alleviate years of solitude as the only being in the waters of chaos. But they were poor companions – they drifted away and could not be found. Atum was alone once again, but he was determined to find his newly created offspring, and so he removed one eye from his face and filled it with his own power, elevating it to the status of a goddess. He then called the Eye his daughter, manifested as both Hathor and Sekhmet.

Atum then commanded Hathor-Sekhmet to scour the universe for signs of his children. Eventually, she discovered Shu

and Tefnut and brought them back to their father. Atum, weeping for joy, embraced them. The tears fell to earth and were transformed into the first human beings. As a reward for her services, Atum placed the Eye on his forehead in the form of a cobra. In this position, he promised, she would be feared forever by gods and men alike.

Hathor, shown here in her benign aspect with cow horns. She is accompanied by the pharaoh Menkaure and the personification of the province of Hu, c.2490–2472BC.

This 4th-Dynasty image is from a tomb at Medum. Grazing geese would have been a common sight in the Delta and the Nile valley. In Thebes they inspired a major creation myth.

original gods. The Thebans did not reject the Ogdoad altogether, but placed Amun as its sole creator: he was the "First One Who Gave Birth to the First Ones". One version of the myth depicts him as a serpent, Amun-Khamutef ("He Who Has Completed his Moment"), living in the waters of Nun. However, it is suggested elsewhere that he emitted a mighty honk, like a goose, which burst into the stillness of the universe, causing a cosmic reaction by which the Ogdoad and Ennead were formed. The bird imagery may have been borrowed from a story that described the world coming into being after a *benu* bird – a heron rather than a goose – laid its egg on the primeval mound (see page 42).

The Thebans developed a distinct theology in which Amun was concealed even from the gods, existing somewhere beyond the natural world. It was thought that a creator had to stand apart from his creation, and Amun, the "hidden" god, suited this role. The texts summarized Amun's mystery and power:

"He is hidden from the gods, and his aspect is unknown. He is farther than the sky, he is deeper than the *Duat*. No god knows his true appearance ... no one testifies to him accurately. He is too secret to uncover his awesomeness, he is too great to investigate, too powerful to know. Manifest one, whose identity is hidden ... as it is inaccessible."

Amun's identity was so secret that anyone who tried to discover his origins suffered instantaneous death. Yet he was also omnipotent, and, as part of the Ennead, he was present everywhere (despite being concealed): as one text put it, "The Ennead is combined in your body: your image is every god, joined in your person." How could Amun at the same time be separate and combined with everything? The Theban response to this paradox was to envisage every god as an image of Amun. They also invented a composite figure that included Re as the face, Ptah as the body and Amun himself as the essential hidden power.

It was at Thebes, the splendid capital of Upper Egypt, that Amun was held in greatest respect. Here, in the spectacular temple complex of Karnak and the smaller but no less impressive one at Luxor, he was worshipped daily by the priesthood and honoured by the population as a whole during his annual festivals. Such sacred mass gatherings were common, but those surrounding Amun were the most magnificent. There were two celebrations – the Festival of Opet and the Beautiful Festival of the Valley. In the latter the cult statues of Amun, his wife Mut and their son Khonsu were taken in procession from their home at Karnak across the Nile to the mortuary temples on the west bank. At the Opet festival, which took place during the second month of the annual flood, the cult statues were carried along the

Sacred Hills

The primeval mound was a common feature in creation myths. As the place where the sun first rose, or where the first divine being was created, the mound fulfilled a vital, if passive, function. Its exact location was never certain, but at each major religious site a facsimile of it was built within the temple boundaries.

Pyramids have been interpreted as replicating the shape of the primeval mound. The earliest, built in step form, was that of King Djoser, constructed at Saqqara (c.2630BC).

At its most basic the primeval mound was nothing more than a pile of sand. At Heliopolis, however, it was a rock venerated as the *benben*, thought to be the petrified semen of the god Atum. The *benben* was the stone upon which the first rays of sunlight fell.

The Egyptians' esteem for the mound found its fullest expression in the construction of the pyramids inside which pharaohs were buried. The pyramid was a representation of the primeval mound from which the dead monarch could launch himself, like the original sun god, into the afterlife. The cap of each pyramid (the *benbennet*) was often gilded, and viewed as an extension of the original *benben*.

Hills could also harbour divine power. Atop a high mountain (called "The Peak of The West"), which overlooked the Valley of the Kings, the goddess Meretseger guarded the dead of Thebes. The daily passage of the sun was also framed by mountains: it rose above an eastern mountain called Bakhu, and, as it approached the *Duat* at the end of the day, it set behind a western mountain called Manu.

---

sphinx-lined avenue which linked the temples of Karnak and Luxor. Here, the priests celebrated the sexual union between Amun and the mother of the reigning king, which took place so that she could give birth to the royal *ka* (spirit). The proceedings culminated when the king himself entered the inner sanctum so that his physical form could receive the *ka*, whereupon he would emerge from the temple as a god.

As Thebes grew in status and wealth, Amun became the nation's supreme creator god. Apart from a brief interlude between 1353BC and 1335BC, when the pharaoh Akhenaten attempted to create a monotheistic religion by abolishing the pantheon in favour of the sun god (see pages 43–45), Amun was worshipped up and down the Nile and in many myths appeared in combination with various other deities.

Khnum and the Origins of Mankind

The Egyptians appear to have had little interest in the origin of human beings. Occasional references here and there, such as the story of Atum-Re's tears (see pages 28 and 33), seem to have been added to the creation myths as an afterthought. However, there was one particularly strong myth concerning human creation which originated in the island shrine of Elephantine, situated by one of the Nile's cataracts just inside the border with Nubia. The priests of Elephantine worshipped a ram-headed deity called Khnum, who was closely associated with the Nile and Egypt's fertile soil.

Khnum was a craftsman. Unlike Memphis's Ptah who thought beings into existence, he created them from clay on his potter's wheel. This is suggested in the Hymn to Khnum found carved on the walls of his temple at Esna: "He knotted the

At every conception Khnum fashioned two models. One represented the new human body, the other the *ka*, or vital essence (see pages 95–96), which continued to exist after its mortal twin had died. These two entities emerged from the womb nine months later as a living child.

In this way Khnum was involved also in the union between Amun and the mother of the king, as celebrated at the Opet Festival (see pages 29 and 51). Inscriptions at Luxor recount how Amun assumed human form in order to impregnate Queen Mutemwiya, mother of the great pharaoh Amenhotep III who ruled between 1391 and 1353BC. According to this myth, once Amun had completed the act of procreation, he instructed Khnum to create models of the new king and his *ka*. The story underlined Amenhotep's divine status and also left no doubt as to which of the two gods was considered superior. In reality, however,

Khnum, the ram-headed god, was worshipped at Elephantine, an island in the Nile just to the north of the first cataract. His association with the flooding of the Nile, an annual event that sparked the yearly cycle of natural activity, befitted his role as a creator.

flow of blood to the bones, /Formed in his workshop as his handiwork, /So the breath of life is in everything." The text goes on to describe how he built the skull and created cheeks, "to give shape to the image". He then furnished the body with a spine to keep it upright, lungs in order to breathe, guts for digestion, and sexual organs to procreate with. Khnum did not restrict himself to the creation of Egyptians, but was responsible for all nationalities. He set in motion the world-wide propagation of the human species as an act of continuous creation, and the Egyptians believed that "without pause henceforth the wheel turns every day".

Khnum at his potter's wheel fashions a person out of clay. The god was described modelling two figures to signify each individual: one represented the *ka* (spirit), while the other represented the physical body. Both came together to create the new being.

31

Khnum was the more ancient, long pre-dating Amun. The priests of Elephantine subtly indicated his seniority by depicting him with corkscrew horns; Amun, too, was sometimes portrayed as a ram, but usually with smooth horns. Sheep with corkscrew horns were the first to be domesticated in Egypt, whereas those with smooth horns belonged to a less distinguished breed introduced at a later stage in the country's development.

Along the whole of the Nile valley, all the way from Heliopolis to Elephantine Island, the process of creation was constantly reinterpreted. The Ogdoad, the Ennead, Amun and Ptah were the major protagonists in creation myths, but numerous other suggestions were put forward during the course of Egyptian history. At one period

in Heliopolis, it was suggested that the sun rose as a "golden child" from a lotus flower on the eternal waters. At another time the sun was represented by the *benu* bird (see page 42). A further version of the Amun story claimed that as a mighty goose he had hatched an egg on the primeval mound, and as the shell fell apart it created a space amidst the primordial waters of Nun in which the world could be formed.

The Egyptians did not worship relics, but where possible each religious centre treasured a physical manifestation of divinity. At Heliopolis they guarded the *benben* stone, which seems to have been regarded as the petrified semen of Atum (see page 30). The *benben* was inscribed with the rays of the sun and was a symbol of both

Serpents

Snakes played a rich and complex role in Egyptian myth, but most often appeared as elemental symbols of chaos and evil – reflecting the real danger posed by their deadly bite.

Fear of snakes was especially justified in the Delta, where they were abundant. The Egyptians wore protective amulets to guard against the risk of being bitten.

The four female deities of the Ogdoad – forces of elemental chaos before the world was created – were represented as serpents. Apocalypse for the Egyptians could be brought about by the great serpent Apophis, which lay in wait to ambush the sun every night. And the sun was destined to become

a snake when the world ended (see opposite).

However, the snake could also have positive attributes in myth. Wadjet, the patron goddess of Lower Egypt, was the most revered of a number of serpent deities. The cobra goddess Renenutet, whose name translated as "the nourishing

The monstrous serpent Apophis was vanquished nightly by the sun god Re, often pictured in the form of a cat. A detail from a papyrus, 1250BC.

snake", was the goddess of good fortune, invoked to ensure bountiful harvests, easy childbirth and a happy future.

creation and resurrection. Its shape clearly related to pharaonic tomb construction: the pyramid came to be seen as a larger version of the *benben* and was capped with a replica of the *benben* itself. The first part of the pyramid to be touched by the morning sun was this pinnacle, which the Egyptians called the *benbennet*; it was also thought to have magical qualities as it provided the initial step on the pharaoh's ascension to heaven where he would join the gods. As spell 508 of the *Pyramid Texts* put it, "I have trodden those thy rays as a ramp under my feet whereon I mount up to Re."

Apophis and the Forces of Darkness

Egyptian creation myths were not exclusively concerned with life and procreation, but also acknowledged the forces of darkness. As in most cultures, the snake, principally embodied in Egypt by the god Apophis, who took the form of a threatening serpent, represented a source of evil, standing for the elemental forces the Egyptians feared. He is frequently portrayed as the enemy of Re on tomb walls and in funerary papyri.

The story of Apophis's birth was told in the second century BC on the walls of Esna temple. It describes Neith (an archer goddess of the Delta) producing Apophis by spitting into the primeval waters – his name meant "he who was spat out". In a variant of the story of the tears of Atum-Re, Neith was the first being to appear on the primordial mound, and it was she who gave birth to the sun. She called to her newborn child but, blinded by his own brilliance, he was unable to see her. As he cried for his mother, he shed the tears that formed humanity. But even as his mother found him, the concept of duality exerted itself: good could not exist without evil, and so just after the sun was created the sinister Apophis was born.

Apophis was the antithesis of the sun – an embodiment of the forces of chaos and evil that churned within Nun's ocean. His huge serpentine coils lurked in the *Duat* every dusk, waiting to destroy the sun god and prevent him from rising over the horizon. Every night Re had to fight and defeat Apophis, but as the serpent was indestructible, his victory was never final.

The defeat of Apophis was an important feature of most pharaohs' tomb inscriptions. Although the snake could not be killed, he was depicted being chopped to pieces, often by Re in the form of a cat, one of the many animals that were held sacred in Egypt (see pages 66–71). His defeat enabled the god-king to rise up and take his rightful place in the sun-god's barque that sailed across the sky.

The victory of the sun in this nightly battle was considered vital to the continuing existence of all forms of life, but was not taken for granted by the Egyptians. If Apophis defeated Re, the world would come to an end. However, it was also important that Apophis should not be destroyed – if either combatant ultimately triumphed, then the balance between the forces of good and evil would be altered and the world would be returned to the chaos from which it had come. As a chapter from *The Book of the Dead* prophesied: "This earth will return to the primeval water, Nun, to the endless flood as it was in the beginning. And in the end there will be no gods or goddesses. Nothing but Atum the Lord of All who made all mankind and all gods." In this final manifestation, Atum was destined to appear as a serpent.

Regardless of whether the universe was seen as springing from Atum's masturbation, Ptah's utterance, the cataclysmic union of the Ogdoad or Amun's goose cry, all the stories make it clear that the Egyptians did not perceive creation as an isolated event. It was an ongoing process that was evident in the arrival of every new day and every new season. Ma'at, the goddess who personified truth, justice and harmony in the cosmos, imposed an unchanging order, and any deviation from her divine command was thought to be profoundly damaging to the social and political fabric of Egypt. Creation was a state of perfection perpetually re-enacted, and its cardinal force, the sun, rose above the Nile every day as a sign and guarantee of cosmic security.

The Sun God

For much of Egyptian history Re was the supreme deity. He regulated the passing of hours, days, months, seasons and years. He brought order to the universe and, as an essential source of energy, made life on earth possible. His daily emergence from the *Duat* symbolized the cyclical nature of creation. But Re's manifestation as the sun was merely one of his many aspects. He was simultaneously a creator, the ancestor of the pharaohs, an agent of daily rebirth and much more besides.

The royal title *sa Re* ("son of Re") was introduced by the pharaoh Djedfere in the Fourth Dynasty – a time when the worship of the sun god was particularly strong. Re was especially celebrated at Heliopolis, Greek for the "City of the Sun". His influence, however, was not limited to this period of Egyptian history – all through the Old Kingdom the Egyptian pantheon was affected by his cult. For example, the kings of the Fifth Dynasty diverted a large portion of state resources to constructing massive temples open to the sun.

Re exerted such a strong influence that most other significant gods were eventually subsumed into the sun cult by the process of syncretism (the fusion of two or more deities to become a single object of worship). For example, Re was combined with the two major creation deities, Atum and Amun, to produce the hybrid entities, Atum-Re and Amun-Re. Thus the sun god came to be worshipped as a creator. Similar amalgamations with other gods expanded Re's dominion.

Re was also the ancestor of the pharaohs, and his role in this guise was even more complex than his fusion with other gods. The Egyptians explained this link between Re and the

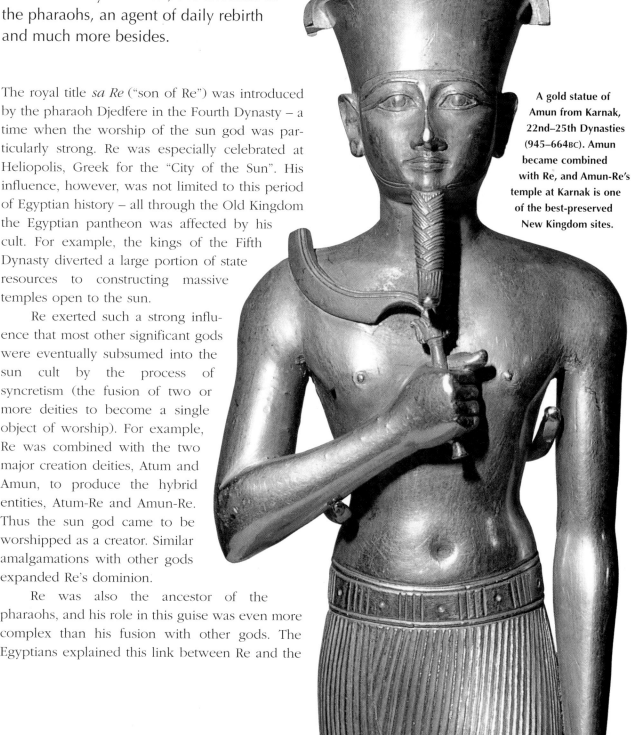

A gold statue of Amun from Karnak, 22nd–25th Dynasties (945–664BC). Amun became combined with Re, and Amun-Re's temple at Karnak is one of the best-preserved New Kingdom sites.

The Destruction of Humankind

Before Egypt had human kings, its ruler was the god Re. In his declining years, angered by his subjects' lack of respect, the god sent his Eye, deified as the goddess Hathor, to take vengeance. The earliest version of this myth was found in Tutankhamun's tomb (c.1323BC), but it may have originated much earlier, possibly in a year when the Nile failed to flood and thousands died.

Hathor, shown here in the guise of the lioness-goddess Sekhmet, was consumed by a bloodthirsty desire to wipe out the human race. Re brought an end to her vengeance by drugging her with vast quantities of beer.

Re, as a ruler of men, was past his prime. As he grew old his bones turned silver, his body gold, and his hair blue as lapis lazuli. But his age did not prevent him from hearing that men were mocking him and plotting to overthrow him. Calling the gods to a secret conference, he asked their advice. Nun, as the eldest, was the one to whom he listened most avidly.

Nun advised Re to punish the blasphemers by scorching them with his blazing heat. However, when Re did this, his victims ran for shelter to the rocks and escaped his fury. Frustrated, Re reconvened the conference. The gods were unanimous: Re should send his Eye in the form of Hathor-Sekhmet (who had previously done Atum good service in finding his children in the cosmic waters; see page 28), to punish mankind.

"No eye is better for this task than yours," concluded Nun. "Let it go forth as Hathor-Sekhmet." Hathor did as she was bidden: she perpetrated a savage slaughter, taking the form of a lioness. By the time that she was recalled by Re, she had acquired an insatiable taste for blood and was determined to return to earth to destroy the rest of humankind.

Re was alarmed. He had meant only to teach people a lesson, not to wipe them out.

While Hathor rested, he sent messengers to Aswan to bring back a consignment of local red ochre. He ordered the High Priest of Heliopolis to pound it. As this was done, the god ordered servant girls to brew barley beer. The two elements were mixed together to produce seven thousand jugs of an intoxicating drink that looked like blood. Re ordered the jugs to be emptied over the fields where Hathor planned her next day of destruction.

Hathor was taken in by the ruse. Flying over the fields, she saw what she assumed to be blood and swooped down for a drink. She drank too much and fell into a stupor. On regaining her senses, she had forgotten her original aim and set off home again, once more the benevolent goddess.

As a gesture of his gratitude, Re decreed that the Egyptian people could drink as much as they liked at Hathor's festivals, in commemoration of Hathor, Lady of Drunkenness.

king in a myth that also accounted for the origins of mankind's destructiveness and inclination to fight in wars.

Re's Ascension to the Sky

At the beginning of time, immediately after the world was created, Re was not a distant figure who dwelled in the sky: he lived on earth as the king of all beings, including the gods. His rule on earth was a paradisiacal time, and his only task was to venture forth occasionally to inspect his domain with a retinue of lesser gods to accompany him. However, Re grew old and began to consider abandoning his duties, which led some of mankind to scorn him and doubt his capacity as a ruler. This attitude infuriated Re, who sent his Eye, in the form of the goddess Hathor, to destroy the miscreants. After avenging himself, he chose to abandon the world and reside in the sky. But his departure was sullied by evidence of further human failing: as he rose above the earth, he saw the people below fighting among themselves, blaming each other for the loss of the sun. Mankind had fallen from grace, and warfare was now endemic on earth.

According to the texts, the responsibility for Re's migration to the heavens lay entirely with humanity. There was no question of divine negligence. One text explained, in the words of the god, the full extent of the blessings that he had brought to Egypt and its people:

This pendant from the tomb of Tutankhamun (1333–1323BC) shows the sun god Khepri (as a scarab) on the celestial boat flanked by baboons with moon discs. The baboon was one manifestation of the god Thoth.

"Words spoken by the Secret-of-Names, Lord of the Universe: I have carried out four good deeds within the portal of the horizon. I made the four winds, that every person might breathe in his time ... I made the great flood, that the poor might be mighty like the rich ... I made every man like his fellow; I did not ordain that they do evil, it is their hearts that destroyed what I had said ... I made their hearts not forget the West [where the sun set and where the dead were buried]."

To mitigate the effects on humanity of his departure to the sky, Re did two further good deeds. First, he instructed the god Thoth to act as his deputy during the hours of night when he himself was voyaging through the *Duat* under the new cosmic arrangements. Thoth was given a great deal of responsibility: his duties were to maintain order and justice on earth, to present people with the precious gift of knowledge in writing (in the form of hieroglyphs) and, above all, to create some light in the night sky (which is why the moon was first created).

Secondly, Re appointed a ruler to take his place as king on earth. To begin with, his choice fell upon gods: his first surrogates were, in turn, the deities Shu (god of air), Geb (god of the earth) and Osiris (lord of the underworld, associated with death and rebirth). But eventually the succession passed on to human beings, providing a convenient mythological lineage for the god-king pharaoh who gained divine status by inheritance (see page 77).

Isis and the Names of the Sun God

The Egyptians were firm believers in magic. The goddess Isis was considered to be especially potent in magical arts (see pages 116–17), and one of her greatest coups came when she persuaded Re to divulge his secret name so that she held power over him.

An incised carving of Isis from the sarcophagus of Rameses III, *c.*1163BC. Her healing powers were put to the service of both gods and people.

"Isis was a clever woman," explained one story, "more intelligent than countless gods ... she was ignorant of nothing in heaven or on earth." She wanted to place herself and her son Horus at the head of the pantheon of gods and the only way to do this was to discover Re's secret name.

One day Isis came upon Re when he was asleep, snoring loudly. From the corner of his open mouth hung a long dribble of saliva which gathered weight and fell to the ground. Isis pounced: scooping up the spittle, she mixed it with clay in the form of a poisonous snake. Then she breathed magic into the snake to make it come alive.

Isis had noted Re's movements and knew that every so often he would leave his palace to go for a walk. Each time, on his route, he passed a crossroads. Isis left her snake there and awaited further developments.

Re emerged for his excursion, and – as Isis had planned – the snake bit him. Re saw nothing, but he felt the poison coursing through him. In pain, he called to the nine gods of the Ennead for help. Re had a fever and was sweating and shivering, but the other gods were helpless: they could do no more that mourn the impending loss of the sun.

Isis then made a dramatic entrance. She could cure him, she said, but only if he would tell her his name. Re refused. She offered again and again, but still he refused. Eventually his agony became so extreme that he could bear it no longer, and he agreed to give Isis the secret, on condition that she should tell it to no one other than her son, Horus. Isis acepted these terms, and speaking aloud the god's true name, she removed the poison. The sun god was cured at once, and Isis and Horus attained the power that they had sought.

This detail from a New Kingdom funerary *stele* (a slab of stone or wood bearing inscriptions or paintings) depicts the sun god as the "Flesh of Re" in the barque that travelled through the underworld each night. Re would take different forms during the day, but for most of his night-time journey he was depicted with a ram's head and a human body.

the vessel. The barque also carried, as passengers, the countless humans who after death had risen to become the blessed dead, and among them Re's descendants, the deceased pharaohs who had joined him in splendour.

Re's daytime voyage was represented pictorially as a journey along the body of Nut, the sky goddess (see page 25). Some myths then describe Re being swallowed by Nut at dusk, and, after travelling through her body during the night, being reborn at dawn – his roseate reappearance at the beginning of the day was said to be symbolic of blood lost at childbirth. Other myths declared that he travelled through the *orouboros*, a massive snake which encircled the universe, tail in mouth.

When Re sank below the horizon at dusk, his journey became hazardous. The *Duat* was divided into twelve chambers or "Gates" – one for every hour of the night – through which Re and his crew had to pass before they could emerge on the other side the next day. Each chamber had specific features, mostly hostile, which had to be encountered and overcome before Re could rise again.

Re's journey through the *Duat* was recorded in three main texts: *The Book of Amduat*, *The Book of Gates* and *The Book of Caverns*. On the precise nature of his passage all the texts differed. In *The Book of Amduat* it was said that Re's first task was to establish land rights for certain gods. According to *The Book of Gates* Re supervised Atum's destruction of his enemies. And in *The Book of Caverns* we learn that Re subjugated three serpents. All these versions, however, were consistent in including two events: a meeting between Re and Osiris, and the subjugation of Apophis and all the enemies of Re, who dwelt in the underworld. These two episodes were essential to secure the sun's reappearance the following day.

The Journey through Night and Day

For ancient Egyptians, night and day were clearly defined periods that each consisted of twelve "hours". This formula never varied. Should the days be longer or shorter, owing to seasonal changes, then each hour expanded or contracted appropriately. This system may have had some confusing practical implications, but at least it provided a framework around which Re's movements could be plotted.

Re sailed across the sky during the day in the *mandjet* (the day-barque), and at night he travelled through the *Duat* in the *mesketet*, also known as the "Boat of Millions". With him travelled a crew of lesser deities who helped to steer and defend

The Meeting between Re and Osiris

Osiris was god of the underworld and the personification of resurrection and reborn kingship. His encounters with Re took place in the *Duat* in the depth of the night. Here, the two gods would embrace as the "Twin Souls" – "Re in Osiris, Osiris in Re" – and replenish each other's life source, to emerge mutually empowered.

This was one important stage in the nightly process that led to Re's rebirth in the morning. However, the climactic event during Re's passage through the underworld was the struggle with the giant serpent Apophis, who represented the forces of chaos. Although Apophis could never be destroyed, Re overcame him each night with the aid of spells, magic and – in some accounts – the cunning of the god Seth.

Each of these two events had special meaning for the Egyptians. The meeting with Osiris affirmed the ability of Re – and so of dead kings – to rise again. At the same time, it may also have served as a political contrivance: at one stage the cults of Re and Osiris were in opposition and their nocturnal unity may have been a means of satisfying both factions. The conflict between the sun god and the serpent was a manifestation of a continual anxiety shared by all ancient peoples: that the sun might fail to rise. There is evidence that solar eclipses provoked a fear that Re had been swallowed whole by Apophis the previous night. In the temple of Karnak at Thebes, and in other centres, priests conducted rituals to assist Re in his struggle. Prayers were offered, incantations uttered, and magic spells recited using the secret names of Apophis. Knowledge of these names was believed to bestow power over Apophis: they

The boat that took Re on his celestial journey each day was thought to be similar to the ordinary craft found on the Nile, of the type seen in this 12th-Dynasty model (1991–1783BC).

The Sacred Scarab

The Egyptians always looked to nature to provide a model for their cosmic imaginings. The activities of the dung beetle provided an ideal allegory for the movement of the sun across the daytime sky.

The dung beetle laid its eggs in a ball of dung that it rolled across the ground to its burrow. Safely ensconced, the eggs would then be incubated by the warmth of the sun's rays. This imagery was irresistible to ancient Egyptians: they saw in the life-cycle of the beetle a microcosm of the daily voyage of the sun emerging from the *Duat* to cross the daytime sky before sinking below the horizon again at sunset.

There were additional aspects to the scarab beetle's symbolism. Inside the warm casing of each dung ball was an egg, which burst open to reveal a larva, causing Egyptians to believe that the insect had created itself. The creature's first flight was also woven into myth as the common motif of the sun god rising up into the sky. In the words of *The Book of the Dead*: "I have flown up like the primeval ones, I have become Khepri ... "

Thus the scarab beetle personified Khepri, the morning aspect of the sun god – and by extension the sun's (and the pharaoh's) rebirth. Khepri is often pictured as a scarab sailing in a boat on Nun, the waters of chaos, or even as a human body with a scarab head.

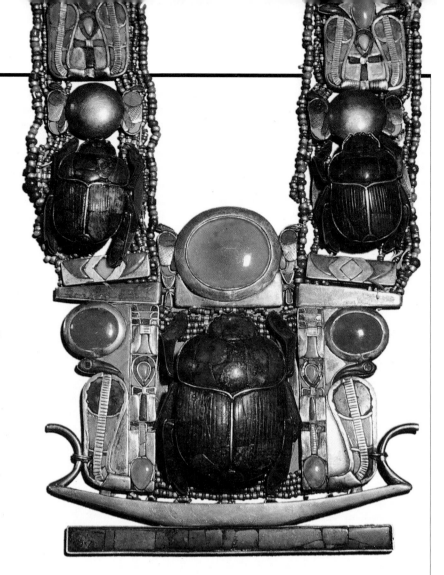

Scarabs were made in various materials – stone and glazed earthenware were especially common – and could have a purely ornamental function, apart from their amuletic properties (see pages 20–21). In the Middle Kingdom they were used as seals, and during the New Kingdom reign of Amenhotep III they served to record important events in the king's reign. Their flat undersides were inscribed with designs referring to a variety of subjects according to their purpose.

Scarabs also played an important role as funerary equipment. Nearly always

Scarabs were particularly popular as symbols of the sun god from the start of the Middle Kingdom (2040BC). This is a pectoral scarab pendant from the tomb of Tutankhamun (1333–1323BC).

fashioned out of blue faience (glazed earthenware), funerary scarabs were large, winged amulets often attached to the surface of a mummy within the bead nets that covered its torso.

Another type of scarab, known as the heart scarab, was inscribed with a chapter of *The Book of the Dead* and was embedded in the bandages of the mummy.

were written in fresh ink on new papyrus which was then burned. Also, according to various texts, wax images were fashioned in the form of a serpent, to be ceremonially spat upon, mutilated and set alight to ward off disaster.

The first glow of dawn signalled a positive response to these prayers and incantations – even though, at this stage, Re had not yet returned to the world. He was in a region called the *Akhet* ("Horizon"), also known as "the place of coming into being", where his power was evident but he could not be seen by the human eye. Seeing the rosy glow at first light, an Egyptian could rejoice in the confidence that the daily cycle was still intact.

The Many Aspects of Re

During his journey across the daytime sky, Re was not represented simply as one god, but took many forms. The sun rising in the east was called Re-Horakhty ("Re, Horus of the Horizon"), an amalgam of Re with Horemakhet (who was himself a form of Horus, as "Horus in the Horizon"). In one Heliopolitan myth Re was also envisaged at dawn as a golden child rising out of a lotus floating on the waters of Nun (the lotus, or water lily, was the emblem of Upper Egypt). More often, however, he was depicted as Khepri, "He Who is Coming into Being", who took the form of a scarab, or dung-beetle. The symbolism of both manifestations was appropriate: the lotus closed its petals every night, opening them only with the sun's appearance; and the scarab beetle emerged from its mound to meet the day. The movement of the sun from east to west was also likened to a scarab beetle pushing its dung-ball along the ground.

Re continued as Khepri until midday, when he reverted to being Re. At this time he was usually shown as a falcon, a bird suitably distinguished both for attaining great heights during flight and for its predatory power. This is Re's most common form. As a falcon, Re is usually depicted bearing a sun disc on his head – an aspect of the sun god that seems to have resulted when he was amalgamated with Horemakhet.

A gilded wooden statue of the falcon god Horus, embodiment of divine kingship. He carries on his head a large sun disc inscribed with a winged scarab representing Khepri, the morning manifestation of Re. This artefact was discovered with one of Tutankhamun's chariots in the antechamber of his tomb (1333–1323BC).

41

Once past his zenith at the end of his daily journey, Re became Atum-Re, the evening sun, in the form of an elderly man. Re was joined with Atum because he was about to enter a world of darkness from which he would be reborn, like Atum, the following dawn. (In some stories Re is also pictured as an ageing king whose flesh was gold, whose bones were silver and whose hair was lapis lazuli; see page 35.) And finally, in the *Duat*, Re assumed the shape of a ram-headed human figure known as "Flesh of Re", his bodily manifestation in the underworld.

In combination with Amun, Re remained pre-eminent in Egypt even after the country had been conquered by invaders. So powerful was this god's hold over the imagination that even the foreign settlers succumbed to his influence. Only once, during the seventeen-year reign of Akhenaten, did Amun-Re's influence falter. At one stroke this heretic pharaoh attempted to promote the sun disk, called the Aten, as a deity, to the exclusion of the rest of the Egyptian pantheon. For a while, instead of being vividly personified, the sun was perceived as a divine abstraction.

The Fiery Phoenix

According to Heliopolitan myth the sun had first risen in the form of a sacred bird called the benu, *popularized as the phoenix by the Greeks. In some accounts the* benu *was a form of the creator Atum, or associated with the* benben *stone that symbolized the primeval mound.*

The *benu* bird is better known to us from Greek myth as the phoenix. It was believed that the bird perished in flames every five hundred years and was reborn out of its own ashes.

The *benu* was also associated with the sacred *ished* (persea) tree, which had solar significance and was protected from Apophis by the Great Cat of Heliopolis, sacred to Re.

In the *Pyramid Texts* the *benu* appeared as a yellow wagtail, a manifestation of the Heliopolitan sun god Atum. Its name translated as "to rise in brilliance". Later, however, in *The Book of the Dead*, it was represented in its common form as the grey heron. Either way, it was seen as a symbol of rebirth and a harbinger of good fortune.

In the form of a heron, it was described as perching above the waters of chaos, occasionally breaking the silence with a cry. The bird's call created a disturbance that set the creation act in motion, determining "what is and what is not to be". This myth reflected that of Amun honking like a goose on the waters of Nun, causing a similar cosmic cataclysm. When the heron settled on the primeval mound it laid an egg which hatched to produce the sun god.

Herodotus recorded it as the phoenix, a bird like an eagle with red and gold plumage that supposedly lived in the Arabian peninsula. There was never more than one alive at any time. When it died, its successor carried the carcass to the sun god's temple at Heliopolis. In another Greek story that encapsulated the *benu*'s mysterious qualities, the phoenix was supposed to set fire to itself and be reborn from the ashes.

The Servant of the Sun

In 1353BC, the pharaoh Amenhotep IV ("Amun is Content") ascended the throne. Many of the surviving portraits depict him as physically distinctive: his spindly shins and weak shoulders were separated by a potbelly and massive thighs. From the top of his odd torso emerged a long, narrow neck, which supported an enormous head, ornamented with big lips and slanting eyes. This highly exaggerated portrayal of the king, with both masculine and feminine features, possibly represented an attempt to promote him as the androgynous primal sun god – "the father and mother of creation". These forms of representation were also applied to portraits of his wife Nefertiti. However unusual his true appearance may have been, he had an extraordinary mind capable of orchestrating a religious revolution.

On coming to power, Amenhotep immediately began to reorganize Egyptian religion. In place of the many gods of the traditional Egyptian pantheon, the new king made the Aten ("Disc of the Sun"), which was devoid of human characteristics, the only deity. Whereas Re had taken a variety of different forms, Aten was depicted only as a disc from which rays extended that terminated in hands holding the *ankh*, the symbol of life.

The first references to the Aten date from several centuries previously. It had become a major deity by the reign of Amenhotep IV's father, Amenhotep III, who himself was known as the "Dazzling Sun Disc". By the time of his son's accession it was widely known as a symbol of the sun and, tentatively, as yet another manifestation of Re. Initially, as a disembodied entity, the Aten continued to coexist with the other gods, albeit in an elevated position. But Amenhotep IV accorded it absolute supremacy. In the fifth year of his reign, the pharaoh symbolically changed his name to Akhenaten (which has been variously interpreted as "One Beneficial to the Aten", "Glory of Aten" or "Incarnation of Aten"). Then he built an entirely new capital on a secluded plain some three hundred and twenty kilometres north of Thebes, in an unpopulated location which had no association with any other god. It is believed that the pharaoh drew the street plan himself. Among other buildings, the new settlement included no less than five

This exquisite wall carving found in the royal tomb at Amarna (formerly Akhetaten) shows Akhenaten officiating in ceremonies of the Aten, the sun disc that was elevated to divine supremacy during his reign. Here he is raising the lotus flower, popular in Egyptian creation myth, to the sun. Akhenaten is often shown with androgynous features.

43

royal palaces and several temples to the Aten. The king called the new city Akhetaten, "Horizon of the Aten"; today it is called Amarna.

The final stage of the Aten's ascendancy came shortly before the new capital was completed, when Akhenaten announced that all Egyptians, and all foreign subjects (predominantly Nubians and Syrians), had to worship the Aten alone.

Akhenaten was supported by his queen, Nefertiti, who was represented in portraiture as extremely beautiful. Together they instituted a wholesale pogrom against the Egyptian pantheon. The most popular sun god, Amun-Re (after whom Amenhotep had originally been named), was a particular obstacle to the virtually monotheistic new cult, and his statues were smashed and his name chiselled off monuments throughout Egypt. To hasten his downfall his priests were thrown out of office, his temples were closed and their great wealth and properties were confiscated by the crown. Anyone whose name included a reference to Amun-Re – as Akhenaten's had previously done – was required to change it. As the new ideology maintained, "Re lives, ruler of the horizons ... returned as Aten."

A few of Akhenaten's subjects resisted. In private, those who denied the Aten's supremacy continued to venerate the old ways, and even in the new capital, some people wore amulets dedicated to other gods. Yet they formed a small community. Within a few years the elaborate panoply of Egyptian religion, with its multiple gods, priests and temples, had been reduced to a single cult led by one individual, Akhenaten. Only he and Nefertiti could communicate with the new sun god and interpret its will.

Akhenaten was a dictator, but he was not necessarily an evil one. In the Aten he promoted a benevolent divinity that was the creator and nurturer of humankind. The cult of the Aten also

A blue-glazed amulet (see pages 20–21) in the form of an *ankh* (the hieroglyph for "life"), *c.*1400BC. The Aten is often shown holding *ankhs* at the ends of its solar rays.

brought a welcome openness to Egyptian religion. Traditionally temples had tended to be dark, mysterious places, shadowed by huge colonnades. Those that were constructed in Akhenaten's reign, on the other hand, were built as spacious roofless courtyards that allowed light to flood in. Within them, beautifully composed hymns were sung in the Aten's honour, celebrating human equality.

Had Akhenaten been more accommodating, his revolution might have survived. However, by focussing on the cult of the Aten to the exclusion of almost everything else, the pharaoh alienated people who wanted to worship old, familiar gods such as Osiris, through whom they could attain rebirth. Inevitably the priests resented their loss of power and revenue. It is also possible that Akhenaten neglected his role as administrator, although there is evidence of military campaigns into Asia Minor during his reign.

When Akhenaten died in 1335BC, the Aten effectively died with him. Following the two-year reign of the shadowy Smenkekare (who was possibly Nefertiti), a young pharaoh called Tutankhaten, possibly Akhenaten's son by a minor wife, ascended to the throne. Tutankhaten abandoned the new capital, restored the old pantheon and began the long and not entirely successful struggle to restore Egypt's material fortunes. As a sign of his good intentions, he changed his name to Tutankhamun. Once more, Amun-Re was in the ascendant.

Akhenaten's presence was systematically obliterated. His city was torn down, his inscriptions were defaced and the old temples were rebuilt. Meanwhile, Re was once again established in the "Boat of Millions", sailing across the heavens: Akhenaten's reign had been merely an aberration in the long rule of the gods.

Akhenaten's Art

King Akhenaten instituted a dramatic development in Egypt's art that long outlived his attempt to elevate the sun disc Aten as the one god. Egyptian art tended towards a flat style that showed people and animals in formal poses (illustrated here). The innovations brought greater realism (as in the carving shown on page 43).

In art before Akhenaten, royal figures had generally been depicted not as they must have appeared but as they aspired to be – grandiose, young and godlike. The new pharaoh changed all that. He issued orders that every living thing be portrayed exactly as it was. His reasons were possibly aesthetic, possibly theological. Certainly, Egyptian art attained a new sophistication. Children were shown as youths, not miniature adults. Birds flew, instead of being stuck, motionless, in the air. Even the king was depicted with Nefertiti and his family, very much at home and with every flaw on show.

The new artistic vogue was most in evidence at Akhetaten (now Amarna), the pharaoh's purpose-built capital. Even though the city was destroyed by later rulers in an effort to stamp out all evidence of Akhenaten's heretical rule, ample evidence has survived. The spectacular painted limestone bust of Nefertiti, discovered in the workshop of the royal sculptor Tuthmosis, is just one of many surviving portraits of the queen. Group images of Akhenaten, Nefertiti and their six daughters (there are no representations of a male heir) are found repeatedly throughout this period. The family is often shown in procession bringing offerings to the Aten. The daughters are depicted playing on the laps of the king and queen in scenes of extraordinary intimacy.

Akhenaten's successors tried to reinstate the old style, but it was impossible to eradicate his new ideas. Ultimately, Akhenaten's contribution to art was to be the most potent legacy of his reign.

This carving on the back of a cedar-wood chair found in the tomb of Tutankhamun (1333–1323BC) exemplifies a partial return to traditionally formal poses after the realism favoured in Akhenaten's reign.

45

HOUSES OF THE GODS

The sheer size and number of Egypt's temples pay homage to the country's ancient gods. Their grandiose pylons (gateways), decorated walls and graceful obelisks glorified the pantheon and symbolized its power. As Egypt's prosperity grew, old temples were embellished and new ones constructed. Thebes, in particular, became an impressive site under the New Kingdom, its hundred-hectare temple complex of Karnak exemplifying the way in which myth and ritual were woven into the very structure of Egyptian sacred architecture.

Left: **Rameses II enlarged the temples at Karnak and Luxor. He often commandeered the monuments of his predecessors by simply having his own name inscribed on them – as in this statue, originally of Amenhotep III, at Luxor.**

Above: **Stone pillars in Egyptian temples were carved to resemble reeds (mostly papyrus) – a reference to the reed-built architecture of the previous age. This example is from the Karnak complex.**

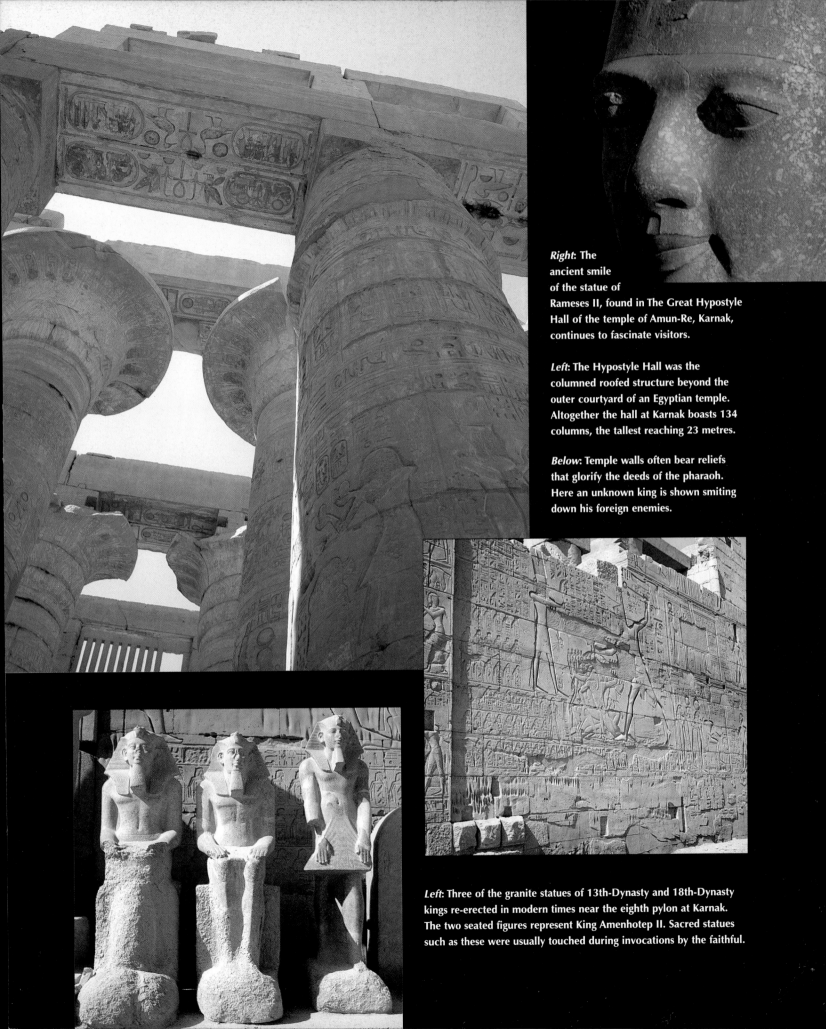

Right: The
ancient smile
of the statue of
Rameses II, found in The Great Hypostyle
Hall of the temple of Amun-Re, Karnak,
continues to fascinate visitors.

Left: The Hypostyle Hall was the
columned roofed structure beyond the
outer courtyard of an Egyptian temple.
Altogether the hall at Karnak boasts 134
columns, the tallest reaching 23 metres.

Below: Temple walls often bear reliefs
that glorify the deeds of the pharaoh.
Here an unknown king is shown smiting
down his foreign enemies.

Left: Three of the granite statues of 13th-Dynasty and 18th-Dynasty
kings re-erected in modern times near the eighth pylon at Karnak.
The two seated figures represent King Amenhotep II. Sacred statues
such as these were usually touched during invocations by the faithful.

Above: The extensive remains of the temple of Isis, originally on Philae Island, had to be moved to Agilqiyya Island (above) during the construction of the Aswan dam to save them from flooding.

Above: Trajan's Kiosk at Philae was commissioned by the Roman Emperor Trajan (AD98–117). Although the Romans had their own architectural style, they still built temples to Egyptian gods.

Right: The temple at Edfu, dedicated to the falcon god Horus, has been well preserved. This impressive granite falcon statue is one of a pair guarding the entrance to the Hypostyle Hall.

Above: At Abu Simbel the two rock-cut temples built by Rameses II must have astonished the traveller Jean-Louis Burkhardt when he found them in 1813. The four seated statues of the king (two are shown above) carved into the front of the larger temple are twenty metres high. The sanctuary was dedicated to Rameses, Amun-Re, Ptah and Re-Horakhty.

Left: The colossal figures at Abu Simbel show the pharaoh wearing the double crown of Upper and Lower Egypt with the familiar *nemes* headcloth beneath. The monument has an air of self-glorification appropriate to a god-king.

Right: Hatshepsut's temple at Deir el-Bahri was the grandest of the female pharaoh's buildings. Its walls record aspects of her reign, especially her trading journeys to Punt, Byblos and Sinai. She was the daughter of Tuthmosis I and she married her half-brother Tuthmosis II. The site incorporates three colonnaded terraces and includes temples to Hathor ("lady of the sky"), Anubis (guardian of cemeteries) and Amun (the Theban creator god).

LIVING WITH THE GODS

Every year, in the second month of the Nile's annual flooding, Thebes swelled to bursting point as tens of thousands of celebrants gathered for the Festival of Opet. This festival, lasting between two and four weeks, and just one of many in the Egyptian calendar, honoured the union between Amun and the mother of the reigning king, which would enable her to give birth to the royal, and at the same time divine, *ka*, or spirit. During that time the statues of Thebes' triad of gods – Amun, his wife Mut and son Khonsu – were taken in ritual procession from Karnak to the temple of Luxor to the south. The spiritual zenith of the celebrations was the moment when the king emerged from the temple at Luxor as a god, his physical form having been united with his divine *ka*. The physical well-being of the worshippers was also attended to, with generous quantities of bread, cakes and jars of beer.

Below: The so-called "astronomical ceiling" of the tomb of King Seti I at Thebes depicts various gods as constellations.

Up and down the Nile, the rest of Egypt's pantheon of gods were accorded similar respect in annual celebrations. The Festival of Bubastis in the Nile Delta, for example, drew crowds of at least 700,000. Indeed, so pervasive was the presence of the gods and goddesses in every aspect of life – from the rising and setting of the sun to the birth and health of children – that the Egyptians had no separate word to denote religion. They, the gods, the world and the planets were all part of the same cosmic order – Ma'at, sometimes personified as a goddess of that name.

Opposite: A *stele*, or pillar, showing the infant Horus under the protective eye of the god Bes, clutching snakes and scorpions to demonstrate his power over harmful forces. Known as *cippi*, these types of *stelae* were thought to have the power to heal.

Within this order, each deity held a particular role, or zone of influence. Thus Thoth was the god of the moon and of wisdom; Hathor was the goddess of love, music and dance, protector goddess of the West and of foreign regions; Osiris was the god of the underworld, of resurrection and vegetation; Isis was the goddess of magic and also shared with Hathor and others the role of symbolic mother of the king. Over time, as the cults of the different deities waxed or waned in popularity, so too the roles of these gods could expand, change in function, or overlap.

The Egyptians identified some of their divinities with the stars which they could see in the night sky. They also mapped constellations and linked their appearance with major events such as the inundation of the Nile or the annual emergence of crops. From the humblest to the highest, the gods were part of the universal order. And by honouring them in their rituals and festivals, the Egyptians ensured that they too were part of the divine dispensation.

The Celestial Domain

During the daylight hours the sky was dominated by Re, the sun god. At night, when he descended to the underworld, the sky became alive with stars, some of which were perceived as deities. The movement of the stars was ordered by the divine goddess Ma'at, just as she regulated the seasons and the relations between the gods and humanity.

Ma'at personified the harmony of the universe. Although she had few temples of her own, statues of her as a seated woman are often found in temples dedicated to other gods. Ma'at represented order, truthfulness and justice, and all human beings sought to live by her ethical rule. The accession of every new pharaoh was greeted as a new beginning and, however effective the rule of his predecessor, the incoming monarch was invariably credited with restoring the spirit of Ma'at to the world. While they recognized their own human fallibility, the Egyptians could always reassure themselves that they were only one aspect of Ma'at. All around and above them, on earth and in the sky, were the gods and goddesses who were equally part of the universal order. They were present in each new season of crops, each new human birth. They were also present in the stars which, in their serene and unchanging motions, provided visible proof of Ma'at's existence.

Observing the Night Sky

The night sky was studied by a group of priests who were known as the "Hour Priests". From observatories set on temple roofs they recorded everything they saw – the movements of constellations, the rising and setting of the sun, the paths of the planets. These priests were not in pursuit of astronomical knowledge for its own sake: what they wanted to determine, in charting the skies, were the patterns of cosmic harmony which would affect life on earth below.

The sky itself was venerated as the great goddess Nut, who took the form of a woman arching over the earth. Every night she was believed to swallow the sun, and every morning she gave birth to him again. (This belief was not considered to be at odds with the myth of Re sailing nightly through the *Duat* in his barque: see pages 38–41.) Because she embodied the night sky, her body was speckled with the stars and constellations which filled the heavens. Nut had no temple or cult dedicated to her – although some of the stars on her body were identified with particular gods and goddesses, and therefore were worshipped as such.

The moon, the largest object in the night sky, was commonly associated with the god Thoth. Described variously as "The Silent Being", "The Silver Aten" and "Beautiful of Night", Thoth was the god of learning and wisdom, and was also

Symbolizing the vault of the heavens, the sky goddess Nut arches her body over the recumbent figure of Geb, god of the earth. Separating the two in this papyrus illustration of *c*.1000BC is the squatting figure of Shu, god of air.

The Egyptian Year

The Egyptian year was initially based upon the lunar cycle and the timing of the Nile's annual flooding. The more sophisticated system that was adopted in due course forms the basis of the calendar that we use today.

In its earliest form the Egyptian year comprised twelve months, each broken down into three ten-day weeks. Day and night were allotted twelve hours each; the length of the hour varied according to the season (although, of course, the variation was only slight as Egypt was close to the tropics). Not until the Ptolemaic period was the sixty-minute hour introduced from Babylonia. Until then, the smallest unit of time was the *at*, or moment.

The year was divided into only three seasons, each of which lasted four months – *akhet*, the period of inundation; *peret*, the time when the flood receded and crops could be planted; and *shemu*, the harvest. Compared to our present calendar with its unequal months, the Egyptian year was a paragon of neatness. However, as soon became apparent, this orderly arrangement did not accord with the reality of the solar year. To correct the discrepancy, five extra days – the epagomenal days – were introduced at the end of the year. These were designated as the birthdays of Osiris, Isis, Horus, Seth and Nephthys, and were celebrated with gala ceremonies.

Under the revised calendar the year started with the first appearance in the morning sky of the star Sirius, whose arrival – on about July 19, according to

Written in hieratic script, a 19th-Dynasty calendar lists propitious days of the year in black ink and unlucky days in menacing red.

the modern calendar – marked the beginning of *akhet*. But even the new system was not without its flaws, for the true solar year is about six hours longer than the allotted 365 days. As a result the calendar and the seasons coincided accurately only every 1460 years. It was not until the Ptolemaic period that the concept of the leap year was introduced – later to form the basis of our own calendar. Until then, the priesthood adopted their own calendar based on a lunar month of approximately 29.5 days to ensure that festivals were celebrated at the right time.

There was, in addition, a further calendar which has been associated with modern notions of astrology. However, although the priests who charted the heavens were to be credited in centuries to come as the fathers of astrology, they did not in fact have a zodiac, horoscopes or planetary houses: these concepts came to Egypt in Ptolemaic times from Babylonia. The calendars that the Egyptian priests kept were of lucky and unlucky days. These were based on mythical events, according to which, for example, a day on which a god was born was considered lucky, and a day on which two gods had fought was seen as unlucky.

Khonsu and the Princess of Hatti

In the late second millennium BC, Egypt was engaged in a long war with the Hittite empire. The conflict was ended finally in 1256BC by the marriage of Rameses II to the daughter of the Hittite ruler, the King of Hatti.

Rameses was captivated by the beauty of his new bride and bestowed upon her the Egyptian name of Nefrure and the title "Great Royal Wife." Shortly after her arrival, however, Rameses was celebrating a festival at Thebes in honour of the god Amun when a messenger arrived from the King of Hatti. He brought bad news. Nefrure's younger sister, Bentresh, was seriously ill and the Hittites were unable to cure her. The pharaoh summoned his top physicians and magicians to ask them their opinion on what this disease might be. When they were unable to reach a diagnosis, he dispatched the royal doctor himself to attend upon the princess.

Three years later this doctor returned home. The princess, he announced, was possessed by evil spirits and only the intercession of a god could cure her. Rameses consulted the priests at the shrine of Khonsu in Thebes, and asked them for their help. The priests in turn put the question to Khonsu, whose

A 13th-century BC statue depicts Rameses II (*c.*1290–1224BC), wearing the false beard and *uraeus* that were familiar symbols of kingship, impassively holding an offering table.

statue nodded its head as a sign that he agreed to be taken to cure the princess.

However, there was one theological problem. In his role as protector of Thebes, the moon god Khonsu had to stay in his city. The priests therefore sought help from the other form of the god, "Khonsu-the-Expeller-of-Demons".

Protected by magical amulets donated by his more senior *alter ego*, Khonsu-the-Expeller-of-Demons set out with his entourage to the Hittite capital. Seventeen months later the statue reached its destination and cured Bentresh on the spot. Bentresh's father, however, was so impressed by the statue's power to heal that he refused to let it go and made a shrine for it in his own kingdom where he intended to keep it. For three years and nine months the statue stayed where it was until the Prince of Hatti was visited by a prophetic dream. In it the statue of Khonsu rose from its shrine in the form of a golden falcon and swooped down at the prince before rising into the sky and heading for Egypt.

The prince realized that he must return the statue, and so he sent it back to Thebes accompanied by a huge tribute. On its return to the city, the statue presented the senior Khonsu with the entire Hittite booty – without having even removed any items of treasure, as recompense for the priests of its own shrine in Hatti.

associated with night. He was linked with the waxing and waning of the moon – one of the primary means of measuring time. He was also a mediator and peacemaker, in which role he was instrumental in resolving the titanic battle between the divine brothers Horus and Seth (see pages 76–84).

As the god of learning, Thoth was associated with every kind of knowledge: scribes in particular saw themselves as "followers of Thoth". This body of bureaucrats prided itself on its service to the state, and in one hymn it was warned that the baboon – an earthly emblem of Thoth – was keeping its eye on errant scribes to ensure that they did not abuse their position by indulging in a little illicit freelance work during office hours.

As the god who oversaw all scientific and literary achievements, Thoth was a lunar librarian, the deity in charge of "the sacred books in the house of life". These books contained the collected scientific wisdom of Egypt. Among them was said to be *The Book of Thoth*, forty-two papyrus scrolls which had supposedly been dictated by the god himself and which covered a wide range of subjects. Four of the papyri contained all of the Egyptians' accumulated wisdom on astrology and astronomy and were required reading for every "Hour Priest". The rest comprised hymns to Thoth and treatises on philosophy and medicine, interwoven with details of religious traditions and ceremonial practices. Tantalizingly, although it is mentioned in many other papyri, no copy of this mysterious book has ever been discovered – one theory holds it that a copy was lodged at the Great Library at Alexandria and perished in the fire there in the fourth century AD.

Thoth was worshipped at Hermopolis where he was believed to be one of the forces behind creation. In Thebes they associated a different god with the moon and with medicine – Khonsu, believed by the Thebans to be the son of Amun. People flocked to his shrine to be healed of their ailments or to have evil spirits driven out. So potent was his statue that it was carried from place to place to cure the sick and the possessed (see opposite).

The Many Facets of Horus

Horus, son of Isis and Osiris, was also a deity with many roles. Represented as a falcon or human figure with a falcon head, he was a god of the sky and god of the east. His left eye represented the moon and his right the sun. In one of the many episodes in the myths of his long struggle with his uncle, the god Seth, it is recounted that both his eyes were torn out and the goddess Hathor had to use her magical healing powers to restore them. In one variant of this story, it was only his left, or moon eye, which was lost. In this version it was not Hathor but Thoth who restored it, acting simultaneously in his various roles as peacemaker, healer and moon god.

Horus embodied the idea of divine kingship and represented the living king, while his father, Osiris, represented the deceased king. Osiris was credited with the annual regeneration of crops made possible by the flooding of the Nile (see

Shown here at approximately twice its actual size, a polychrome glass fragment that may once have served as a furniture inlay depicts the god Horus in his most common manifestation as a falcon. From the Graeco-Roman period.

55

page 108). Orion, the constellation with which he was identified, appeared in the sky just before the flood arrived in July. Among the myths about the conflict between Horus and his brother Seth, one told about how Osiris was trampled to death by Seth in the guise of a bull, and was restored to life by the goddess Isis, who was both his sister and his wife. Seth, too, had a place in the heavens. In one version of the myth, Horus chopped off Seth's foreleg and flung it into the night-time sky where it hung as the Great Bear constellation.

A direct parallel to the family of Isis, Osiris and Horus was provided by the goddess Sopdet (Sothis in Greek), her husband Sah and their son Soped. Sopdet was the personification of the dog star Sirius, and hence had an important role in the Egyptian calendar as marking the start of the season of inundation. Like Osiris, with whom he was identified, Sah is associated with Orion. In the Old Kingdom *Pyramid Texts* Sopdet is described as uniting with Osiris to give birth to the morning star – that is, the planet Venus.

The "Hour Priests" also observed in the night sky the "Ikhmu-Seku", "The Imperishable Stars", which seem never to set when seen from the latitude of Egypt. These are the circumpolar stars, which the Egyptians believed to be the souls of those who had achieved perfection in the afterlife. By the Middle Kingdom, Egyptian astronomers had also identified "The Stars Which Know No Rest", a term that referred to the five planets nearest to earth. Three of them were named after Horus: "Horus who limits the two lands" (Jupiter), "Horus, bull of the sky" (Saturn) and "Red Horus" (Mars). The other two were named "Segebu", a god associated with Seth (Mercury), and "God of the Morning" (Venus), linked with Osiris.

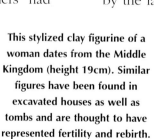

This stylized clay figurine of a woman dates from the Middle Kingdom (height 19cm). Similar figures have been found in excavated houses as well as tombs and are thought to have represented fertility and rebirth.

Gods of Fertility and War

A number of gods were linked with growth and fertility. Hapy, who presided over the Nile's flood, lived in the cavern at the southernmost cataracts on the Egyptian border. He was associated with the creator god Khnum who controlled the gates which were thought to have held back the flood and who gave the order when they were to be raised to unleash the benevolent waters upon Egypt. Min, who was celebrated riotously in festivals at Coptos and Akhmim in Upper Egypt, was the god of male sexual potency. And the god Bes, despite his extraordinary appearance as a bow-legged, lion-maned dwarf, sometimes depicted clad in a motley of animal skins and feathered headdress, was a protective god of the household and of childbirth. Behind, or rather under, all was Osiris, god of the underworld (*Duat*). As the god of rebirth in the *Duat*, he was considered responsible for each new season's crops, his spirit manifest in every green sprig of growth.

Some gods and goddesses, in attending to other aspects of life, were at the same time seen as deities of war. Among the goddesses were Sekhmet (the lioness-goddess known as the "powerful one"), Neith ("mistress of the bow, ruler of the arrows") and the two Syrian deities, Astarte and Anat, worshipped in Egypt by the late second millennium (see page 65). A major Egyptian warrior god, also associated with hunting, was Anhur, whom the Greeks identified with their own war god Ares. The name Anhur means "he who brings back the distant one": he was believed to have left Egypt for Nubia and returned with Mehit, his lioness consort who was associated with Sekhmet. That Sekhmet was regarded as the daughter of Re (in combination with Hathor as the

Eye of Re; see page 35) served to bolster the idea that Anhur was a son of Re.

Montu was another god of war. Worshipped in Thebes, he was depicted as a falcon-headed god whose headdress bore the disc of the sun. He was seen as the conquering spirit of the pharaoh and as such was venerated at the city of Tod, to the south of Thebes. The measure of his power was reflected in the Middle Kingdom pharaoh Amenemhat II's gift to Montu's priesthood – four chests full of treasure from Syria, the Aegean and Mesopotamia, as emblems of Egypt's supremacy in foreign lands.

As Egypt came in contact with other, more martial civilizations, so it adopted some of their divinities of battle in preparation for war. One such was Reshep, a mace-wielding deity from the Levant, who rose to prominence following Egypt's colonization of Syria and Palestine during the second millennium BC.

Another was Ba'al, infamous in the Old Testament because he killed and devoured human beings. He was accepted into the Egyptian pantheon as a god of thunder and the battlefield during the second millennium BC when the Egyptians were in conflict with the Hittites. At one cult centre he was associated with the Egyptian god of chaos Seth (see pages 77–84), probably because one of Seth's functions was to be a god of thunder.

Thoth and the Eye of Horus

One account of the long battles between Horus and Seth (see page 76) describes how Horus lost both his eyes; another claims that it was his moon eye that was torn out. The eye was found and restored to its original position by Thoth – an action symbolizing restoration of the cosmic order.

Horus was resting beside an oasis when Seth crept up on him in the form of a black boar. As Horus slept, Seth ripped out his left eye and flung it beyond the edge of the world. Horus awoke and retaliated by ripping off Seth's testicles. But there was nothing that he could do about his eye, which seemed lost forever. Meanwhile, deprived of its moon, the night sky sank into blackness.

A bronze statuette from the Ptolemaic Period depicts ibis-headed Thoth, the divine scribe credited with the invention of speech and writing. The god was believed to play a part in the judgement of the dead, recording with his scribal palette the results of the weighing of the deceased's heart (see pages 104–105).

Thoth came to the rescue. Ever the peace-maker during the conflict between the two gods, he scoured the chaos beyond the world's confines until he discovered the missing eye. It had been shattered by its fall, but Thoth pieced it together and restored it to its owner. The Eye of Horus was thereafter represented by the *wedjat* amulet.

57

The Divine Protectress

Among Egypt's female deities were goddesses of fertility, child-bearing and healing, but their roles extended far beyond those of nurturers and protectors. Sekhmet and Neith were venerated as powerful and belligerent forces; Isis was the supreme magician; and Ma'at symbolized the order of the universe. Hathor was celebrated as the goddess of love, music and dance. So great was the fame of many of these goddesses that they were recognized well beyond the confines of Egypt.

The most enduringly popular of all goddesses was Isis, whose cult was adopted enthusiastically by the Greeks and Romans. Her influence in the Roman Empire reached as far as Britain, where, even today, many bridges on the River Thames bear her image. Isis spanned many aspects of Egyptian culture. With Osiris, she was said to have helped to civilize Egypt, taught the people how to farm, given them the secrets of medicine and instituted the custom of marriage.

A wall painting from the Theban tomb of Nefertari, wife of Rameses II, shows the goddess Isis leading the dead queen by the hand. From New Kingdom times Isis was commonly identified with the cow goddess Hathor, whose horns she wears here.

Isis may possibly have evolved from an early fertility goddess. Archaeological finds have shown that the early Egyptians worshipped a goddess whose potbelly clearly demonstrated her fecundity. During Graeco-Roman times, Isis was the most revered of female deities, and her cult rivalled even the new Christian religion. Associated with Osiris, she was at the same time his sister and his wife. (The pharaohs themselves often married their own sisters.)

As his sister, Isis helped Osiris in the struggle with their brother Seth, bringing him back to life by taking the shape of a kite and flapping her wings to put breath into his body after Seth had used his trickery to kill him. As she did so, the revived god impregnated her, and in due course she gave birth to a son, Horus. Isis's act of resurrection frequently appeared on coffins, which bore the image of a bird enfolding the dead in its wings.

As the mother of Horus, Isis was regarded not only as a link between royalty and the gods, but also as having a maternal role that extended to the population at large. She became venerated as a protector of children, and her name was often called upon in magical spells to cure childhood ailments. In a typical example, to heal a scald, a plaster of human milk, gum and cat hair was applied to the sore spot while an incantation told Isis that her son was in the desert with no water to soothe him. The expected response from Isis was that she would alleviate the pain with a mixture of saliva and urine – "the Nile flood between my thighs", as it was euphemistically described.

A squatting woman goes into labour with the assistance of twin images of Hathor, one of two major deities invoked in childbirth (the other was the hippopotamus goddess Taweret). This Ptolemaic relief comes from Dendera, north of Thebes.

Having given birth to Horus at Khemmis in the Nile Delta, Isis watched over her son assiduously so that he might grow up to avenge his father. And just as the legends of Horus and Seth spread, so too did Isis's attributes grow more numerous. She was respected as the devoted wife, the ideal mother, a healer, a resurrector, a deity of children and fertility and, finally, a goddess of magic and cunning, "more clever than a million gods". Notable among her feats was the occasion when she tricked Seth into proclaiming his guilt in front of the Ennead and her discovery of the secret name of Re (see page 37).

Hathor, Goddess of Love and Fertility

The goddess Hathor was accorded almost as much respect as Isis and, like Isis, was given many identities: she could be shown in human form, or as a cow, or a lioness, or even occasionally a snake or a sycamore tree. She was also Mistress of the West – the land of the dead – and a funerary goddess. As the Eye of Re, or Atum-Re, Hathor could also take the form of the destructive lioness Sekhmet.

In her cow form, she was a goddess of fertility. As such she had a special association with royal births: she, as well as Isis and Mut, was seen as the symbolic mother of each pharaoh. The pharaoh was sometimes portrayed drinking the milk of the goddess Hathor in reaffirmation of his divine right to rule Egypt. There was a further connection between Hathor and the pharaoh: Hathor was Horus's wife, and each pharaoh was considered the earthly embodiment of Horus. As the son himself of a pharaoh, each pharaoh was entitled to be described as "the son of Hathor". However, the pharaoh was equally considered the son of Isis as her cult grew in popularity.

As the sworn enemy of evil, Hathor shook her favourite musical instrument, the sistrum (a kind of rattle), to drive away malign influences. Like Isis, Hathor was a healing goddess, and at her cult centre in Dendera mud-brick cubicles were con-

The Cat Goddess

One of the most popular goddesses was Bastet, whose name means "she of the ointment jar". Bastet was originally depicted as a lioness wielding a sceptre, but over time she dwindled in ferocity to become a cat-headed goddess holding the musical instrument known as a sistrum.

The cat, far from being a symbol of power like the lion, was seen as a free-spirited embodiment of household entertainment. Although most often linked with royalty, cats were favourite pets in even the lowliest household. Like Hathor, Bastet was considered to be a daughter of the sun god, and was a national deity of protection. She was celebrated at lively festivals with dancing, music and sistrum-playing at her cult centre, Bubastis.

Hatshepsut, the best known of Egypt's few women pharaohs, kneels to receive the benediction of the seated Amun-Re and the lion-headed goddess Sekhmet in this carved, 15th-century BC relief from the temple of Karnak in Thebes.

The Egyptians recognized the potential for destructive behaviour in their gods and goddesses: Hathor provided a particularly vivid example of this when she adopted the form of the leonine, vengeful Sekhmet, with a compulsion to destroy the whole of humanity. Sekhmet was also associated with plague, and was sometimes seen as the consort of Ptah, the Memphis creator god.

The opposite natures of the lion and the domestic cat are seen in the following myth, where Hathor is identified as Sekhmet until she returns to the care of the sun god. The story is also typical in encompassing the several aspects of Hathor.

Hathor, as the Eye of Re, rebelled against the sun god and fled to the deserts of Nubia. Thoth, the eternal peacemaker, was sent to find her, disguised as a baboon. But when he discovered her, she did not appear either in her normal form as Hathor, nor as Sekhmet, but as the cat goddess Bastet. Thoth used all his charm to make her homesick, recounting stories of Egypt and the life she had left behind. But all this was to no avail, and instead of being charmed, Bastet suddenly turned into Sekhmet, the furious lion goddess. Thoth redoubled his efforts – finally to good effect. Soothed by his words, Hathor agreed to return with him to Egypt, where she was greeted at the border by crowds of well-wishers.

However, their difficulties were not over and a serious danger faced them before they could return. Shortly before they reached the end of their journey, Hathor fell asleep, and Apophis, the serpent of chaos, came to attack her. Just as he was about to kill her, Thoth saw what was happening and came to her rescue by shaking her awake. They now entered Heliopolis in triumph, whereupon the Eye of Re reunited herself with the sun god.

Other Goddesses

Initially associated with funerary rites, Neith, an ancient archer goddess of the Delta, was symbolized by a shield and crossed arrows. She was identified with Athena by the Greeks, and with Diana by the Romans. A fearsome but righteous deity, she was a wise mediator often described as a divine mother figure, and sometimes regarded as the mother of Sobek, Isis, Re and even Apophis. In one myth, she is credited as the first being to appear on the primeval mound. At times, she could even intercede with the Ennead, and she played a judicial part in the epic battles between Horus and Seth.

Satis, a goddess associated with the island of Elephantine, guarded the southern frontiers of Egypt. But her protective role was not exclusively martial. With her cult centre situated at the point

The Festival of Bastet

The festivals held annually at the Delta city of Bubastis in honour of the cat-headed goddess Bastet were among the best-attended in Egypt. Colourfully reported by Herodotus, these events were widely held to be fabrications until archaeologists discovered evidence to confirm that they actually happened.

By the Late Period, Bastet's festival was one of the most popular in the Egyptian calendar. For ceremonial purposes the town of Bubastis – eighty kilometres northeast of modern Cairo – was best approached by water. "They come in barges," wrote Herodotus of the festival, "men and women together, a great number in each boat; on the way, some of the women keep up a continual clatter with castanets and some of the men play flutes, while the rest, both men and women, sing and clap their hands. Whenever they pass a town on the river bank, they bring the barge close in-shore, some of the women continuing to act as I have said, while others shout abuse at the women of the place, or start dancing, or stand up and hitch their skirts. When they reach Bubastis, they celebrate the festival with elaborate sacrifices, and more wine is consumed than during all the rest of the year."

Herodotus recorded at least 700,000 people – "excluding children" – arriving in similar fashion to pay their respects at the red granite temple which had been erected in honour of the goddess. Again, according to Herodotus, "Cats which have died are taken to Bubastis where they are embalmed and buried in sacred receptacles." Thousands of the dead creatures were mummified and interred in underground galleries here and at other sites so that they might carry their owners' messages all the more swiftly to the realm of the gods.

The sheer scale of the festival seemed incredible to early Egyptologists. But in 1887 an archaeologist called Edouard Naville, excavating the site, discovered that Herodotus had indeed spoken the truth. He uncovered the site of Bubastis's main temple, the catacombs of mummified cats, and a number of pharaonic shrines which proved that even the highest born venerated Bastet.

A bronze from early in the 1st millennium BC shows the cat goddess Bastet shaking the rattle-like instrument known as the sistrum.

The Wives of Seth

Following Seth's long and unsuccessful battle with Horus for the Egyptian throne, the goddess Neith suggested to the council of gods that Seth be awarded a loser's prize: the "foreign" daughters of Re were offered to him as his wives. The involvement of these divine consorts, Anat and Astarte, may be connected with Seth's own affinity with the foreign gods Ba'al and Reshep.

One day as Seth was walking by the Nile, he came across the goddess Anat, bathing in the stream. He changed himself into a ram and raped her. But Anat could only be impregnated by divine fire, and so her body expelled his semen with such force that it struck him in the forehead, making him

With evil intent, Seth, the troublemaker of the Egyptian pantheon, approaches Anat in the shape of a ram.

dangerously ill. Seth was relieved of his punishing headache by Re, whom Isis sent to cure him.

In another myth, of which only a part has ever been found, the gods of Egypt were in conflict with the sea god, Yamm, and were coming off the worst. Yamm demanded tribute of gold, silver and lapis lazuli, which was duly brought to him by the goddess Renenutet. However, having received these treasures, he became greedy for more, and insisted on further tribute. He threatened that, if his demands were not met, he would enslave every god in Egypt. In despair, Renenutet sent to Astarte, who was famed both for her beauty and her ferocity. The messenger, in the shape of a bird, begged Astarte to carry the extra tribute to Yamm. Reluctantly, Astarte agreed. But when she reached the shoreline, her fiery nature got the better of her and she began to taunt the sea god. Alternately outraged by her impudence and bewitched by her beauty, Yamm demanded that he be given Astarte as well as the treasure. The goddess Renenutet retired to deliberate with the gods, who acceded to the sea god's demands and furnished Astarte with a dowry consisting of Nut's necklace and Geb's signet ring.

Seth, however, rebelled against losing his beautiful wife. Tantalizingly, the remainder of the story is lost. But the outcome, surely, was that, whether by force or by guile, Seth overcame the sea god, saved Egypt's pantheon from slavery, and returned from the adventure with Astarte.

where the annual inundation first becomes apparent, she was given a share of the credit for this event. And because of her association with the Nile's sacred waters, she was seen too as a purifier of the dead.

Over the centuries, the native Egyptian goddesses were joined by foreign deities. During the rule of the Hyksos – immigrants whose name simply means "rulers of foreign lands" – who appear to have entered Egypt peacefully during the eighteenth to sixteenth centuries BC from the area of Palestine, three striking deities were added to the pantheon:

the two martial goddesses Anat and Astarte, and a goddess of love, Qudshu (see below).

Egypt's goddesses enjoyed a popular appeal which the gods – for all their pomp and importance – never quite achieved. Indeed, when the closure of all the temples had been ordered by the Roman Emperor Theodosius in AD384, one continued to function – the temple of Isis at the city of Philae, near Aswan on the Egyptian-Nubian border. Until around AD535 this remained the centre for a cult of Isis which had been powerful enough to challenge early Christianity for religious supremacy.

Foreign Goddesses

During the mid-second millennium BC, Egypt assimilated a wave of immigrants mostly from neighbouring countries, who added further deities from their own mythologies to the Egyptian pantheon.

Found in the palace of the Assyrian kings at Nimrud in what is now Iraq, this ivory plaque is thought to represent the goddess Ishtar, the Mesopotamian cousin of the Syrian divinity Astarte.

Of all the additions to the Egyptian gods at this time, none featured more prominently than the two warlike goddesses Anat and Astarte, and at a later period Qudshu, goddess of sexual love. Anat, a deity of battle, was – in a twist of the Isis myth – both sister and husband to the Middle Eastern god Ba'al, who was worshipped in Egypt as an aspect of Seth. She is also depicted with Min, Egyptian god of fertility – an

association that emphasizes the pronounced sexual nature of her cult. In Egypt she was held to be the daughter of Re. She was also linked with Hathor, as both were associated with foreign lands, both had a potential for aggression, and both were sometimes presented in a distinctly sexual manner.

Astarte was also seen as a daughter of Re and additionally as a daughter of the creator god Ptah. She was particularly

associated with horses and chariots, and is sometimes portrayed naked on horseback.

Qudshu was, by comparison, a benign goddess. In Egypt she was believed to be a consort of Min, as well as being linked with Hathor. Unlike Anat or Astarte, she carried only symbols of reproduction, such as the lotus. But the powerful sexuality she demonstrated was not to be doubted, for Qudshu rode naked on a lion.

Sacred Animals

Even in the time before dynastic rule in Egypt, animals were accorded a high degree of respect, and worshipped in totem form at sites throughout the country. As the culture developed, these animals were seen as representatives of the gods, sacred because of their divine associations rather than as objects of worship in their own right.

Writing in 450BC, Herodotus claimed that all animals, "wild or tame, are without exception held to be sacred". However, the Egyptians did not revere animals because they were sacred in themselves, but rather because certain creatures were believed to contain the divine essence or physical manifestation (the *ba*) of certain gods. In worshipping an animal, they worshipped the power of the deity contained within or represented by that animal. Even so, such veneration of certain species could cause acute local antagonisms, as was amply demonstrated by the neighbouring towns of

One of the many gate-keepers of the *Duat*, known as "He who Protects Himself", depicted in a 20th-Dynasty tomb.

Oxyrynchus and Cynopolis. The Oxyrynchans held sacred the Oxyrynchus fish, whereas the Cynopolitans, who considered dogs to be holy, ate the sacred fish as a part of their diet. On being requested by the Oxyrynchans to give up eating their holy fish, the Cynopolitans not surprisingly refused. The Oxyrynchans duly held a banquet at which the main dish was roast dog.

Such instances of outright conflict were no doubt rare, but what this account does indicate is the popularity of animal cults, particularly in the Late Period down to Classical times. Among the major cult sites were Elephantine and Mendes associated with rams, Bubastis and Saqqara with cats, Hermopolis Magna with baboons, and Kom Ombo with crocodiles. The falcon, emblematic of Re as well as Horus, Montu and Sokar, was adopted by many towns, as an emblem and as a cult object, for its predatory speed. Crocodiles were chosen for the dread that they could instil in an enemy, as were snakes. Some towns picked defensive motifs: the mongoose, for example, would give protection against snakes. Dogs, cats and geese were seen as guardians of the home. As the gods became associated with certain creatures (for example, Horus with the hawk, Amun with the ram and goose, Thoth with the baboon and ibis), offering a mummified animal rose in popularity as a way to attract the chosen god's favour. And to make sure the animal delivered its message to the god, it was mummified with almost as much care as humans were.

At the town of Hermopolis, where Thoth was the predominant god, ibises were reared specifically for sacrificial purposes. A supplicant would approach the priests and, for a suitable payment, choose an ibis from its compound. Once slaughtered and elaborately mummified, the creature was placed in the catacombs. The sheer volume of the business was staggering – in the Serapeum at Saqqara, archaeologists found the mummies of one and a half million ibises and hundreds of thousands of falcons.

By the Graeco-Roman period, the sacrificial process had its own set of formalized rules. For example, given the difficulty of raising falcons, it was held that another bird mummified in its shape would suffice. And although Egyptians mummified every conceivable kind of animal, from mongooses and shrews to crocodiles and bulls (even, in one recorded case, an egg), their choices could be restricted by cost. It was a small expense to immortalize a shrew, whereas to mummify a crocodile was a different matter altogether. In the case of larger animals the sacrifice and mummification were generally performed on behalf of the whole community.

Animals in the Afterlife

In some cases the animals were considered more than just spiritual messengers. The Egyptians loved their domestic pets and looked forward to their company in the afterlife. Many tombs show pictures of owners with their dogs, often the saluki

This mummified cat, sacred to the goddess Bastet, was found at Abydos. In the Late Period it became common to preserve the animal's remains in her honour, and an extensive cat cemetery has been uncovered at Bubastis, her cult centre in the Delta.

breed, known as the "Hound of the Pharaohs". Cats, however, were the favourite pets, in part because of their roles as enthusiastic mousers, and in part because of their hostility to snakes. A favourite theme for tomb paintings was the cat of Re defeating Apophis, the serpent of chaos which stood in the way of the sun's daily rebirth.

Herodotus was amazed by the protection that Egyptians extended to their cats during a house fire. "Nobody takes the least trouble to put out the blaze for it is only the cats that matter. Everyone stands in a row ... to protect the cats which nevertheless slip through the line, or jump over it, and hurl themselves into the flames. This causes the Egyptians deep distress. All the inmates in a house where a cat has died a natural death shave their eyebrows." When a cat died, according to Herodotus, it was mummified and buried in the town of Bubastis, and X-rays of some of the cat mummies found there suggest that they were ritually strangled before being buried.

The vital part played by cattle in the agricultural economy made them central to existence – and a select few, the Buchis, Mnevis and Apis bulls, and the cow-mother of the Apis bull, which was worshipped as Isis, were thought to contain the essence of the particular deity that they represented. The power was instilled in only one animal, and through the generations. So the most important of these, the Apis bull of Memphis, represented Ptah when alive and Osiris when

Sacred Bulls

The bull was venerated at sites throughout Egypt, each of the worshipped bulls being thought to contain the essence of a god, transferred through successive generations. The most significant and sacred bull was the Apis bull of Memphis.

The bull, like the lion, was an emblem of power and as such was frequently associated with both gods and pharaohs. Sacred bulls were kept in the greatest splendour, paraded at religious festivals, consulted for their oracular powers and, on their death, accorded a mummification fit for a pharaoh.

The most famous of sacred bulls was Apis, which resided in a temple compound at Memphis, and was seen as an embodiment of the god Ptah when alive, and of Osiris after death. Another sacred bull was Buchis, linked with Montu, god of war. Its cult centre was the town of Armant, south of Luxor, where successive generations of bulls were mummified and placed in a special cemetery in coffins whose lids weighed as much as fifteen tonnes. The Buchis bull embodied both Re and Osiris. Mnevis, the sacred bull of Heliopolis, was also associated with Re.

Every bull was chosen for its markings. It was required that Mnevis be entirely black, with tufts of hair on its body and tail. Buchis had to possess a white body and black face, whereas Apis, according to Herodotus, was to be black with the mark of a vulture on its back, a white diamond on its forehead, double hairs on its tail, and a scarab-shaped mark under its tongue. It was believed, too, that Apis must be born of a virgin cow which had been inseminated by a flash of lightning – but this stipulation, understandably, was more often honoured in the breach than in the observance.

Herodotus related an episode which had seemingly occurred in 525BC when the Persians conquered Memphis amid great bloodshed: the Persian king, Cambyses, arrived to inspect his conquest only to find that the survivors were celebrating. On being told that he had captured the city on the same day that a new Apis had been found, he burst out laughing and had the bull roasted at a banquet. This terrible act of disrespect was held to be the cause of every evil that befell the Egyptians from that time on.

A painting from the coffin of a 21st-Dynasty Theban priest shows the Apis bull, worshipped as a manifestation of Ptah, and also identified with Osiris.

dead; the Mnevis bull of Heliopolis embodied Re; and the Buchis bull of Armant was sacred to Montu, and contained the *ba* of Osiris and Re.

According to Herodotus, Apis was no ordinary bull, but had always to fulfil a host of exact specifications (see page 68), among them precise markings on its body. But these specifications did not indicate that such a beast was rarely found, for by the Graeco-Roman period the rules were elastic, and any one of the marks was considered sufficient. In the last resort, a black spot on the tongue would do instead of a beetle marking. Once located, the calf was treated like bovine royalty: it was given golden blankets and its own harem of cows. When it died, the bull was ceremonially mummified and buried with gilded masks and jewellery and all the pomp accorded to a pharaoh. In the account of a Nineteenth-Dynasty *stele*, "it happened that the majesty of the Apis departed to heaven, to rest in the embalming house under Anubis that he might mummify his body. The children of Horus raise him up while the lector priest recites glorifications." Thereupon the whole city entered a period of prolonged mourning while the priests of Apis began a search for the bull's successor. Diodorus, a Greek from the first century BC, recorded the event: "When they have found [a calf], an end is put to all further ... lamentation and such priests as are appointed for the purpose lead the young ox through the city and feed him for forty days. Then they put him into a barge wherein is a golden cabin and so transport him as a god to Memphis ... During the forty days before-mentioned none but women are admitted to see him, and these, naked, are placed full in his view. Afterwards they are forbidden to come into sight of this new god."

In addition to their religious significance, cattle had practical importance for Egyptians as draught animals and sources of meat and milk. This harvest scene comes from the Theban tomb of Menna in the 18th Dynasty.

Crocodiles, Hippopotamuses and Lions

Other weighty creatures of veneration were the crocodile, the hippopotamus and the lion. In many places the crocodile was kept as a living representation of the god Sobek, a symbol of pharaonic might and also an ally of the god of chaos, Seth. The foremost shrine was in the town of Crocodilopolis in the Fayum, a famously verdant area of Egypt where the Delta of Lower Egypt meets the valley of Upper Egypt. In myth the crocodile had a dual nature: on the one hand it was menacing and dangerous, on the other, benign and protective. In *The Book of the Dead*, a quartet of crocodiles was one of the many menaces that the dead encountered, whereas in the *Pyramid Texts* Sobek was described as the god who restored the deceased's eyesight and acted as a guide to the throne of Osiris. The crocodile was considered the friend of both Osiris and Horus. In one of the many myths about hostilities between Horus and Seth, the crocodile was credited with carrying Osiris's body on its back to the shore, after his defeat at the hands of Seth (see page 76). In another, the creature was seen as the protector of Horus, for when he was a child his mother, Isis, had delivered him to the Nile knowing that the crocodiles would protect him from harm.

Like the crocodile, the hippopotamus was characterized as both good and evil. A deceptively ten years of his reign. During his long and glorious rule he erected a huge number of statues to the lioness goddess, Sekhmet, often portrayed as a woman with a lioness's head. The pharaohs Rameses II and Rameses III kept lions which they took into battle to inflict casualties on the enemy.

In the underworld, the lion was deified as Aker, an earth god who presided over the western and eastern horizons of this realm. His cult can be traced back to Early Dynastic period. Aker is often portrayed in the form of two lions, positioned back to back – known as the lions of "Yesterday" and "Tomorrow" – who lay at the exit and entrance. Sometimes this pair were given the heads of men, and immortalized as the guardian sphinxes (see opposite).

Hunters prepare to spear a hippopotamus in this painted relief from the Old Kingdom period. Hunting was a popular motif in Egyptian art, although the pursuit of big game seems to have been largely the prerogative of the king and wealthy nobles.

placid beast, it was easily roused to anger. It was this angry creature that constituted one part of the hybrid Ammut, Devourer of the Dead, who waited in the Hall of Judgement in the underworld to devour those who were unfit for eternity. And yet hippos were also representative of Taweret, goddess of childbirth, an altogether more benign role.

As in most cultures, the lion was seen as an emblem of power. Considered a great hunter for having overcome the lordly creature, the pharaoh Amenhotep III reported that he had killed over one hundred lions with his own bow in the first

Animals as Oracles

Many animals in Egyptian myth also served an oracular function, whether as messengers from the afterworld or as representations of a particular power or quality. In this latter role, their responses to given stimuli were carefully monitored, judged and pronounced upon. The bull of Apis was particularly respected in this regard: the Roman author Pliny described a particular instance in which the sacred bull exhibited his powers of divination. "Then the youths who accompanied him sang hymns in his honour, while the Apis appeared to understand all, and to desire that he be worshipped. Suddenly the spirits took possession of the youths and they spoke prophecies."

The bull was also said to foretell events on its own initiative. In the first century BC it predicted the death of the Roman general Germanicus when it refused to eat out of his hand. In the same century its bellowing announced that Egypt was about to be invaded by the Emperor Augustus. A bull's passing from one room to another in a temple was held to be significant, and people sleeping there received its utterances in their dreams. (This animal was not the only source of insight in temples: even the cries of children playing outside were thought to hold replies to questions asked within.)

The national veneration of animals reached a peak in the last centuries before the banning of the old gods, when the country was under Greek and later Roman control. Herodotus reported that anyone found guilty of intentionally killing a sacred animal was sentenced to death. Four hundred years later, Diodorus witnessed an incident in which a Roman official accidentally killed a cat and was promptly lynched by a mob.

By the fourth century AD many of Egypt's native animals were getting scarcer. As one Roman chronicler noted of the hippopotamus, "now they are nowhere to be found, since, as the inhabitants of those regions conjecture, they became tired of the multitude which hunted them". The near extinction of the hippopotamus was followed by that of the lion and the leopard. It was as though their vanishing mirrored Egypt's own decline.

The Enigma of the Sphinx

This mythical creature was generally portrayed with a human head wearing a head cloth and the reclining body of a lion. It was associated with the power of the king and the sun god.

An inscription on the base of one late-first-millennium BC sphinx states proudly: "I protect the chapel of thy tomb, I guard the gate. I ward off the intruding stranger. I hurl thy foes to the ground and their weapons with them. I drive away the wicked one ... I destroy thine adversaries in their lurking place."

The sphinx – a Greek term perhaps derived from the Egyptian *shesep-ankh*, or "living image" – could have the features of a pharaoh; or it could be ram-headed, like the sphinxes representing Amun, which once formed an avenue linking the temples of Karnak and Luxor.

The greatest of all the sphinxes sits before Giza's second largest pyramid. Constructed by the pharaoh Khephren (*c.*2520–2494BC), it stands 20 metres high, 73 metres long, and was carved from a single rock outcrop. Between its paws lies a *stele* of granite inscribed on the orders of Tuthmosis IV who ruled more than one thousand years after Khephren. It tells how, as a prince, Tuthmosis, in a dream, was told by the sphinx that he would become the next pharaoh (see page 88).

Sphinxes were sometimes depicted trampling the enemy to death. This image is an elaboration of their role as protectors of the king.

Known as the "alabaster sphinx", this recumbent New Kingdom statue lies within the walls of the temple of Ptah at Memphis.

A DIVINE MENAGERIE

The Ancient Egyptians were surrounded by domestic animals and wildlife. The balance of nature was seen as essential to the maintenance of order in the universe, and mythology reflects the close kinship between gods, creatures and humankind. That animals held the key symbolic role in the worship of the gods is therefore not surprising. The diversity of this animal pantheon reflects the fecundity and richness of Egypt's fauna. Creatures of the land, sea, river and air all played their part.

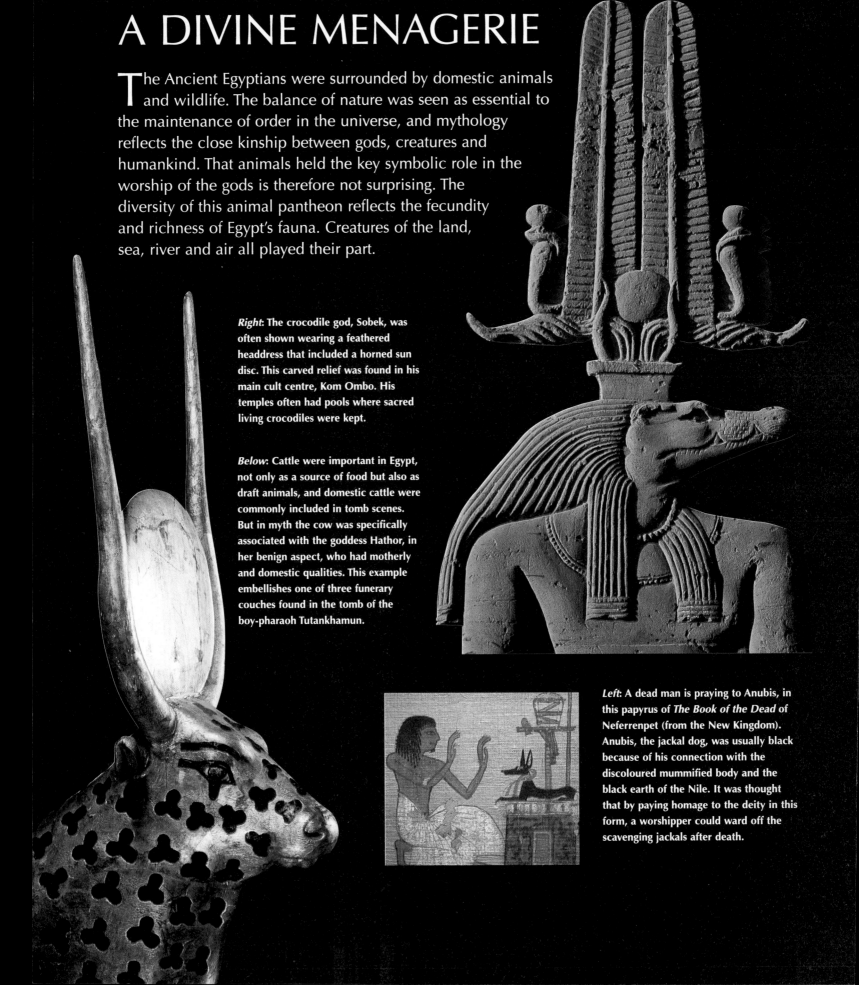

Right: The crocodile god, Sobek, was often shown wearing a feathered headdress that included a horned sun disc. This carved relief was found in his main cult centre, Kom Ombo. His temples often had pools where sacred living crocodiles were kept.

Below: Cattle were important in Egypt, not only as a source of food but also as draft animals, and domestic cattle were commonly included in tomb scenes. But in myth the cow was specifically associated with the goddess Hathor, in her benign aspect, who had motherly and domestic qualities. This example embellishes one of three funerary couches found in the tomb of the boy-pharaoh Tutankhamun.

Left: A dead man is praying to Anubis, in this papyrus of *The Book of the Dead* of Neferrenpet (from the New Kingdom). Anubis, the jackal dog, was usually black because of his connection with the discoloured mummified body and the black earth of the Nile. It was thought that by paying homage to the deity in this form, a worshipper could ward off the scavenging jackals after death.

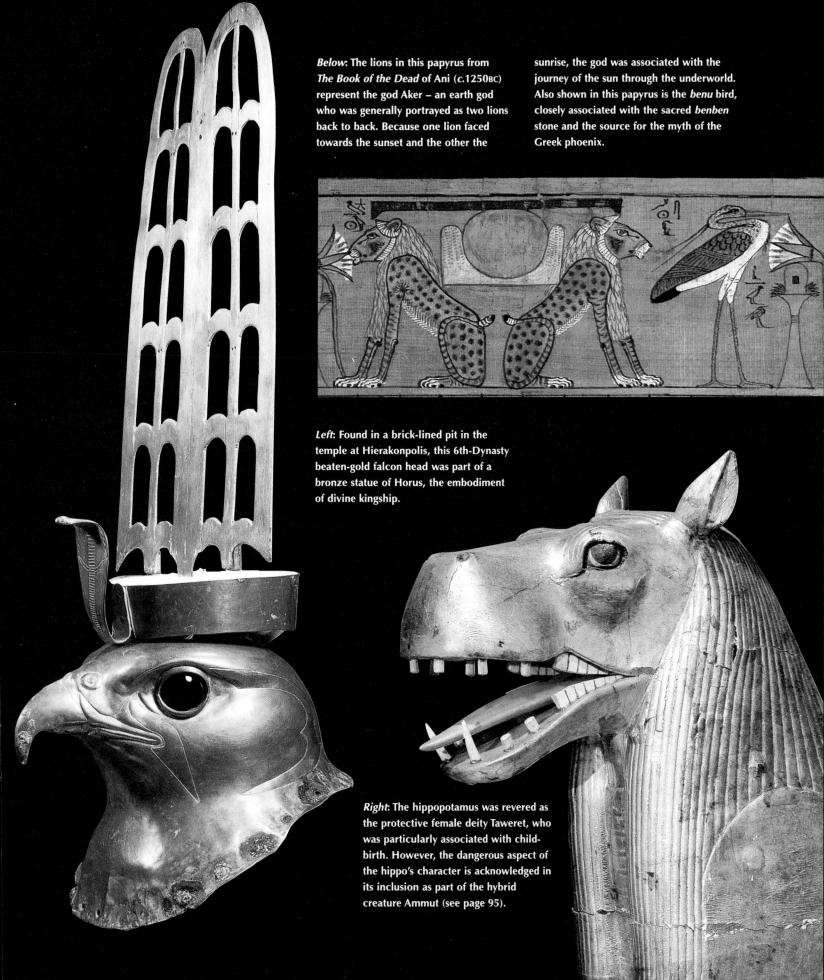

Below: The lions in this papyrus from *The Book of the Dead* of Ani (*c.*1250BC) represent the god Aker – an earth god who was generally portrayed as two lions back to back. Because one lion faced towards the sunset and the other the sunrise, the god was associated with the journey of the sun through the underworld. Also shown in this papyrus is the *benu* bird, closely associated with the sacred *benben* stone and the source for the myth of the Greek phoenix.

Left: Found in a brick-lined pit in the temple at Hierakonpolis, this 6th-Dynasty beaten-gold falcon head was part of a bronze statue of Horus, the embodiment of divine kingship.

Right: The hippopotamus was revered as the protective female deity Taweret, who was particularly associated with childbirth. However, the dangerous aspect of the hippo's character is acknowledged in its inclusion as part of the hybrid creature Ammut (see page 95).

THE MIGHTY SONS OF RE

The gods ruled over Egypt, supreme on earth and in heaven. First, there was Re, god of the sun; after him came Shu, his son, the god of the air who lay between the sun and the earth; and then lordship passed to the earth god Geb, the son of Shu, and thence to his own son Osiris.

Even gods, however, engaged in terrible rivalries. Osiris was murdered by his brother Seth, and a titanic struggle ensued between the usurper and Osiris's son, Horus, before Horus at last achieved permanent ascendancy. This was the founding myth of Egyptian kingship, because Horus was the divine prototype for the pharaoh. And the king, on his accession, was regarded as "the living Horus", a kind of earthly god, combining the mortal and the divine.

Such ancestry bestowed a unique privilege – it meant that the pharaoh was king not only of Egypt, but also of "the world". For in the divine sense, there could be only one king; the Egyptian term for king was not a word that was ever used for a foreign potentate, no matter how mighty. Such a ruler would be described only as "great chief". And naturally, all great chiefs paid tribute to the pharaoh. Or so royal propaganda insisted: visiting ambassadors might have brought courtesy gifts, but the records would always claim that these were tribute for the son of the gods. Many New Kingdom tomb scenes depict foreigners bowing low before the tribute that they have offered: it could not be otherwise.

To be king in Egypt meant more than just ruling over the land and its people. The pharaoh was also the one true intermediary between the heavens and his mortal subjects. He alone could perform the rituals that ensured the continued beneficence of the gods. He might allow others to deputize for him in this task (indeed, he had to, as despite his divinity he could not be everywhere in his domains at once), but no priest – far less a commoner – could claim any shred of religious authority in his own right.

With the pharaoh in place between gods and mortals, ordinary Egyptians could live at peace with each other and, more important, in harmony with divine forces. Sometimes disorder threatened, and hard times of civil strife and foreign invasion put their cherished system of belief in Ma'at's order under agonizing strain. But for more than two millennia, the sons of Re, on earth as in heaven, kept Egypt safe in their embrace.

Above: **King Rameses III greets the goddess Hathor in the tomb of the king's son, Prince Amunhirkhopshef. As a deity himself, Egypt's ruler could consort with other gods on near-equal terms.**

Opposite: **Wearing the red crown of Lower Egypt, King Montuhotep (2061–2010BC) is greeted by the god Montu, in a wall painting from Montuhotep's temple at Deir el-Bahri, 11th Dynasty. Kingship and godhood were inextricably intertwined.**

The Conflicts of Horus and Seth

The story of Horus and Seth is set at the beginning of Egypt's long history. When the mighty sun god Re relinquished his rule on earth, he left as his successor his son Shu, who was succeeded by his son Geb, and in turn by *his* son Osiris. Following his marriage to his own sister Isis, Osiris taught humankind the arts of agriculture and civilization, and proved a wise and just ruler. He brought abundance and prosperity to the land and Egypt flourished as never before. But the golden age was all too brief. For there was terrible jealousy within the god's own family. His younger brother, Seth, burned with envy at Osiris's success and ruthlessly plotted against his life.

A Late Period bronze of the jackal-headed Anubis. The god embalmed the dismembered body of Osiris, for which service he became patron of mummifiers.

Osiris, so full of goodness, found it impossible to see evil in others, and made no effort to protect himself from Seth's malice. Stories of how Seth murdered him differ: according to Plutarch's widely-told version, Seth sealed Osiris in a chest and threw it into the Nile (see page 82); according to another account, he turned himself into a raging bull and trampled Osiris into the dust.

In any event, Seth was not satisfied with a simple killing. Still consumed with jealous rage, he hacked the body to bits and scattered the pieces throughout the land. So it was that the soul of his brother left the world of the living and crossed into the darkness of the underworld. He was the first living thing to die; and as such, it was only fitting that in his afterlife he should command the land of the dead, the kingdom of the West. Seth, safe in the knowledge that Osiris had left behind no son to avenge him, settled down to enjoy the kingdom he had usurped.

Isis, sister-wife to Osiris, was wild with grief. But she was also enterprising and resourceful: using all her skills of divination and magic, she scoured the land of Egypt with the help of her sister Nephthys until she had pieced together her husband's body. (In later times, cult temples all over the land marked sites where dismembered parts of the murdered god were found.)

Isis then sought out the jackal-god Anubis. He was generally regarded as the son of Nephthys, the fourth of the children of Geb and Nut; some claimed that his father was Osiris. Whatever his ancestry, Anubis sought to help Osiris by embalming the remains, the first time that such a feat had been accomplished. Anubis, as the inventor of mummification, came to be regarded as a god of great service to the dead.

Isis, using her own magic as well as the skills of Anubis, was able to resurrect her dead husband for just the amount of time needed to impregnate herself with his seed. She then sought refuge at Khemmis in the Nile Delta, where she gave birth to Horus, far from the reach of his jealous uncle. While the boy was an infant, he was cared for by Isis herself and by the cow goddess Hathor, who served as his wet-nurse. As soon as he was old enough, Isis brought her child before the council of the assembled gods to demand the return of his birthright: the throne of Osiris.

The meeting was long and stormy. Re himself was unwilling to allow the lordship of the earth to pass from mighty Seth to a mere boy; but most of the other gods were impressed by the evident justice of Horus's case. As Shu, god of air and the eldest son of the creator, put it: "Justice should triumph. We should give Horus his throne." The scribe god Thoth declared his agreement: "That is a million times right."

Re was not convinced by their decision, and was more than somewhat disgruntled that any other god should dare to oppose his will. Isis was also

The Divinity of the Pharaoh

From the beginning of pharaonic times, Egypt's kings were revered not only as royal, but divine. Their godhood served as a link between the land, the people and the deities who ruled the universe.

In the hierarchy of Egyptian religion, only the king was permitted to make offerings to the gods: there could be no other mediator between earth and heaven. Although such work might well be delegated to the high priests, it was understood that a priest only deputized for the king, having, in theory, no authority of his own.

The goddess Hathor greets King Seti I in a scene that originally embellished his Theban tomb, c.1290BC.

Each pharaoh was a god from birth. Though the queen was recognized by all as his human mother, the idea that he had been sired by Amun-Re, incarnate as his royal father, was just as widely accepted. When the pharaoh had his own son, the same principle of divine incarnation would ensure that godhood was passed down through the dynasty.

The coronation rituals further reinforced this concept. And at death, the king became wholly divine: no longer taking the living form of Horus as ruler, he became one with Osiris in the underworld, while at the same time joining his father Re in his ascendancy over all things.

All this was the most natural of arrangements and a matter of simple, if wonderful, fact. None doubted the irresistible logic: "God is our king; the king is a god." The pharaoh's divinity, almost like a written constitution, established the Egyptian state as an entity sactioned by the law of humankind and the gods.

Seth, Lord of Disorder

In very early times, Seth was worshipped at his cult centre, Naqada, and because he was associated with the frightening desert sandstorms of the region, it was important to appease him. He ultimately became a lord of misrule and chaos, the god of storms, the enemy of Horus and the organized world that Horus stood for. Indeed, that enmity was part of the Egyptian order, a darkness against which the divine light could flourish.

Like most Egyptian gods, Seth was often pictured with the head of an animal – usually the strange "Seth beast", an imaginary creature with a vague resemblance to an ant-eater. Sometimes he was depicted as one of the animals considered to be "unclean" by the Egyptians – such as the hippopotamus or the pig.

For all his villainy, Seth's antecedents were impeccable: as the son of sky goddess Nut, he matched in divine status his brother Osiris and his sisters Isis and Nephthys (the latter was also one of his wives). Indeed, his strength and rank among the gods gained him Re's support during much of his bitter struggle with Horus. After his defeat on earth, he journeyed with the sun god during the hours of the night, defending him against the serpent Apophis.

Seth's immense strength and his forceful sexuality guaranteed him the veneration of at least a minority of mortals. Although never a popular god, he did have his good points: an appeal to Seth, the lord of chaos, might help keep bad weather away. Indeed, at one point in Egypt's history, he enjoyed a period of general worship and respect, during the Nineteenth and Twentieth Dynasties (1295–1069BC).

But Seth was always a dangerous god to venerate. The following dynasties characterized him as the god of harm, and by late in Egyptian history he had generally come to be regarded as the personification of evil-doing.

Seth is depicted in this basalt carving with his sister and wife Nephthys at his side. For most of Egyptian history, Seth was lord of chaos, a god to be carefully placated.

proving a very able advocate. At one point in the wrangling, Seth became so angry with Isis's cunning pleas that he threatened to kill a god for each day that Isis remained at the divine court.

"Let us cross over to the island in the middle of the river," said the sun god, "and tell the ferryman to deny passage to Isis, or any who may resemble her." Nemty, the divine ferryman, duly rowed all but Isis to the island, and returned to the mainland where he waited while the gods enjoyed a meal during a break from their disputations. After a time, Isis appeared on the bank, disguised as an old crone. "Ferry me across," she begged. "I am taking food to the cowherd who has been working on the island for the last five days."

At first, Nemty refused, even though he had no suspicion that he was talking to Isis. But the bribe of a golden ring soon changed his mind, and Isis entered the camp of the gods. Once again, she changed her shape, this time taking on the appearance of a beautiful young woman dressed in widow's weeds. Seth, always a roué, at once approached her.

"Why are you here, and who are you?" he asked, in a bantering tone. "O great lord," answered Isis, "I come to seek justice. For I was the wife of a cowherd, and bore his son. Then when my husband died, the boy went to take over his father's herd. But a stranger came, and seized our cattle for himself. When my young son protested, the stranger threatened him with a beating. Please, help me restore my son's inheritance." Seth waxed indignant. "How can a stranger seize the cattle while the son is still alive?" Isis had got what she wanted. Turning herself into a kite, she flew to a nearby tree and cackled with laughter at Seth's hypocrisy. "O Seth, you have judged yourself." This time, the other gods, including Re, agreed. Together, they prepared to crown Horus as rightful lord of the earth.

Seth, though, was far from willing to accept the verdict. He may have lost his crown, but he was still unbeaten; and to prove it, he challenged Horus to the first of a series of combats. With Re's approval, the two gods transformed themselves

In the prow of Re's solar barque, Seth leans forward to spear the dangerous serpent Apophis (see page 32). Despite Seth's evil reputation, his enormous strength was greatly valued by Re, who relied on his protection each night as he passed through the *Duat*. From the Hirweben's *Book of the Dead*, 21st Dynasty.

into hippopotamuses, and fought in the waters of the Nile. "He who survives three months," declared Seth, "shall be given the throne."

So the battle commenced. But once more Isis intervened – though this time to little effect. She quickly contrived a magic harpoon from a piece of copper and some yarn, and hurled it at Seth. But the churning water where the beast-gods were struggling confused her aim, and her first throw struck Horus. Instantly she used her magic to retrieve the weapon, and threw it once again. This time, the barb penetrated Seth, who rose to the surface with a cry of pain. "O sister," he wailed, "why are you always my enemy? I am your brother: let me go."

Isis could not resist her brother's plea, and at once removed her harpoon. This was more than Horus could bear. He burst from the water in so great a rage at his mother's change of heart that he actually cut off her head with one stroke of his copper knife. He took hold of the head, then marched to the mountains.

79

But Isis was, after all, the Mistress of Magic, and so, unperturbed, she turned her body into a flint statue and walked over to join the watching assembly of the gods. When Re was told exactly what had happened, he was beside himself with anger at Horus. While Isis restored herself to normal form, the gods scoured the earth for the miscreant.

It was Seth who found him, sound asleep in the shade of a shenusha tree in an oasis in the western desert. Seth at once leapt upon his nephew and tore out both of his eyes. Leaving Horus to his terrible pain, Seth buried the eyes in the desert, where they took root and grew into two fine lotus flowers. Then Seth returned to Re – and denied he had ever seen Horus.

One by one, the other gods abandoned the search. Only the goddess Hathor, who had wet-nursed the baby Horus, refused to give up; and it was she who found the eyeless god the next morning. With milk taken from a passing gazelle, she anointed the bleeding sockets and restored Horus's sight. Then she took him with her to the assembled gods and told them about Seth's appalling deeds.

But this time, Horus had also put himself in the wrong: he had attacked Isis with extreme violence, and even though his mother had forgiven his irrational action, Re refused to show favour. He ordered a truce between Horus and Seth.

Lotus flowers blossom across the walls of the temple of Seti I at Abydos, just as they burst forth from the torn-out eyes of Horus after Seth had buried them in the desert. Shortly afterwards Horus's injuries were miraculously healed. The lotus was regarded as a symbol of rebirth.

An Intimate Encounter

Seth's hatred did not diminish, and Horus soon found himself contending once again with the older god's superior strength and immense capacity for dirty tricks. Against these qualities, Horus had only two genuine weapons: a burning sense that justice was on his side, and a mother whose cunning and command of magic proved enough to tip the balance.

Isis's help was especially useful on an occasion when Seth subjected his nephew to an outright sexual attack. In ancient Egypt, semen was thought to flow through all the veins of the body, and was considered both potent and dangerous – so much so that the word for semen was similar to the word for poison. A god's semen was considered particularly powerful.

After decades of fighting between Horus and Seth, the other gods were growing increasingly weary of the destructive rivalry, and there came a time when Re flatly ordered it to end: "Be at peace together, and cease your quarrelling."

Making a show of accepting the edict, Seth attempted to befriend Horus and invited him to his home. In due course, night fell; a bed was prepared, and the two gods settled down together. When Seth thought that Horus was asleep, he attacked him sexually to show his dominance over his younger rival.

But Horus was ready, and caught Seth's seed with his hand. At once he ran to Isis, crying, "Look what Seth has done to me!" Isis, who understood the dangers from Seth's semen, at once cut off her son's hand – and threw it into the Nile. (Of course, she quickly replaced it with another.)

Then she prepared a counter-attack. She took some of Horus's own semen and took it to Seth's garden, where she sprinkled it over the lettuces, the god's favourite vegetable. Sure enough, the next morning Seth came to his garden to pick and eat the lettuces, and in the extraordinary way of gods, he became "pregnant" with the seed of Horus.

The next time the two rivals appeared before the council of gods, Seth began to boast once more of his might and skill. He seemed to be making a powerful impression – until Horus asked the gods to call out to his seed and that of his uncle. In response, Thoth laid hands on Horus, and summoned the seed of Seth, but it answered only from the river. However, when in turn he touched Seth and called for the seed of Horus, it answered from within the god. Thoth then summoned the seed to Seth's forehead, where it appeared – to Seth's great rage – as a golden sun. This proved the dominance of Horus over his uncle.

When Seth came to his garden to pick lettuces, his favourite vegetable, he was impregnated by the semen of his nephew Horus, sprinkled there by Isis.

The Final Battle

Already, the struggle between the two had lasted many decades (according to the gods' particular reckoning of time). But Seth demanded one last challenge. "Let us each build a ship of stone," he said, "and race each other down the Nile. The winner will have the crown of Osiris."

Horus built his ship first, out of stout pine; but then he plastered it over to make it look as if it had been made of stone. When Seth saw it, he used a mighty club to knock off a whole mountain top, from which he built a much larger ship of solid stone for himself. Of course, when the two boats were launched, Seth's vessel immediately sank to the bottom. But Horus had little time to laugh: Seth at once changed himself into a hippopotamus, charged at Horus's ship and dashed it to pieces. Undaunted by this, Horus prepared to

81

Plutarch's Version

By Graeco-Roman times, one at least of Egypt's goddesses had acquired a greatly expanded repertoire. Isis, mother, healer and arch-magician, appealed enormously to peoples all around the Mediterranean and beyond. Naturally, from this worship there grew a great demand for new tales of the goddess.

Plutarch, the Greek historian and biographer who lived from c.AD46 to AD120, was one of many writers glad to oblige. From Egyptian sources, which he mixed with a little Greek legend and no doubt a few ideas of his own, he came up with a colourful account of the trickery Seth used to murder Osiris.

In Plutarch's version, Seth ordered the making of an exquisitely-crafted chest, to the exact height and width of his brother. Then he threw a great banquet for Osiris, at which he displayed the chest to the admiration of all. It should belong, said Seth, to whomsoever it might fit; and one by one the guests tried the chest for size. But none matched its measurements – except Osiris himself. And the moment the unsuspecting king lay in the chest, Seth and his fellow-plotters promptly nailed the lid shut, sealed it with molten lead, and cast the chest upon the waters of the Nile Delta.

Isis at once set off to find her husband's body. But by the time she learned where Seth had put the great chest, it had floated far out to sea. It finally came to land at Byblos in the Lebanon. There, the washed-up chest gave root to a sapling which magically grew into a vast tree big enough to enclose Osiris and his coffin within its trunk. Impressed by the size of the tree, the King of Lebanon had it cut down and used as a pillar for his new palace – with Osiris still within.

In time, of course, Isis tracked the coffin down, and to the astonishment of the king and his court, cut open the great roof-pillar and removed her husband's body.

The tree, Plutarch adds, lending credibility to his tale, was preserved for many years in Byblos and worshipped there.

Highly decorative chests were valued items of Egyptian furniture. This ornate example belonged to the Lady Meryt and was found in the tomb that she shared with her husband Kha (c.1400BC).

harpoon the hippopotamus-Seth. But the other gods intervened to stop him.

Thus another battle was over, leaving everything still unresolved. Despairing of a solution, Horus went to see Neith, the revered goddess of wisdom, in her Delta city of Sais. "Please," he begged her, "let judgement be made. For eighty years, Seth and I have stood before the tribunal of the gods, and we are no nearer a decision. I have won the day a thousand times, yet Seth refuses to give in, and never pays the slightest attention to what the gods say to him."

When the other gods heard Horus's plea to Neith, they agreed that he was justified. Besides, their own patience in dealing with the dispute was by now completely exhausted. At last, Thoth suggested to Re that he apply for advice to Osiris him-

Isis, mother of Horus, used all her skills to ensure her son's victory over Seth. This relief, depicting Isis, is from the tomb equipment of Yuya and Thuya, the great grandparents of Tutankhamun, c.1380BC.

self, in the Beautiful West, his kingdom of the underworld. And, accordingly, a messenger was dispatched to the realm of Osiris.

After a long and perilous journey into the realm of the dead, the messenger returned with Osiris's reply. Not surprisingly, the god supported his son Horus. But he was also greatly angered that justice had not already been done for the boy: why, asked Osiris, should Horus be cheated?

Re was irked at being addressed in such a manner, and sent the messenger on his journey westward again with a haughty answer. This time,

83

A tomb painting of Horus, in his customary, falcon-headed form, decorates the tomb of Rameses I. The god wears a double crown, which represents his right to rule over both Upper and Lower Egypt. This right was finally won at the end of his long battles with Seth.

Osiris's rage knew no bounds. "Here in my kingdom of the dead," he wrote, "there are many powerful demons: should I send them into the land of the living, to return here with the stolen hearts of evil doers? For I am much stronger than you: sooner or later, even the gods must come to sleep in my Beautiful West."

Osiris's threat resolved the matter. In solemn conclave, the gods agreed that Horus should inherit the lordship of the earth. Re ordered Isis to bring Seth in chains before him, which she willingly did. "Seth," asked Re, "do you still claim the throne of Osiris?" By this time Seth was ready to concede. "No, great one. Let Horus be summoned and given his father's throne."

The long dispute was finally over. The young Horus was given the crown of Egypt, and all the earth rejoiced. As for Seth, Re had something to offer by way of recompense. "You may join me in the skies as my son, and god of storms," he told the loser. "Your thunder and lightning will terrify people for eternity."

The Divine Order

Taken as a whole, this myth was – and is – a powerful evocation of the tension and conflict between, on the one hand, the forces of order, as exemplified by Osiris and Horus; and, on the other hand, their dark counterparts, the chaos and confusion represented by Seth (see page 78). There were times in Egypt's long history when Seth won a temporary victory; but it was in the interest of all people, for the sake of peace and prosperity, to support the successors of Horus.

And the successors of Horus, of course, were the pharaohs. So it was that the human king of Egypt took the name of Horus (given to him on his accession) and added it to his own, which not only set him clearly among the gods, but also announced him to be the earthly representative of the forces of divine order.

The Horus-Seth myth reflects issues of kingship that were rarely discussed openly in Egypt. Young Horus is portrayed as a vulnerable candidate vying for the position of supreme ruler, who in the end is victorious over his uncle, Seth, who represents chaos. Although successful usurpations were rare, Egypt needed a central myth to discourage what it most feared – the violent transference of power. The triumph of Horus was regularly enacted as a ritual drama in temple ceremonials, so that Egypt remained united: "The white crown (Upper Egypt) is the Eye of Horus; the red crown (Delta) is the Eye of Horus."

84

The Earthly Power of the Pharaoh

Since the pharaoh was a god, it followed that he had absolute power on earth. However, despite the trappings of divinity, ordinary human politics ensured that there were sometimes plots against his power. Assassinations and usurpations were rarely mentioned – such chaotic possibilities were too dangerous to contemplate – but treachery was by no means unheard-of.

One famous document, *The Instructions of King Amenemhat*, purporting to be the last testimony of the king, set out a bleak and Machiavellian view of Egyptian power-politics:

Beware of subjects who are nobodies,
Of whose plotting one is not aware.
Trust not a brother, know not a friend,
Make no intimates, it is worthless.
When you lie down, guard your heart yourself,
For no man has adherents on the day of woe.
I gave to the beggar, I raised the orphan,
I gave success to the poor as to the wealthy;
But he who ate my food raised opposition,
He to whom I gave my trust used it to plot.

Apart from the ever-present risk of treason, Egypt at the height of its civilization was simply too large and complex for one man to exercise sole power. There was the priesthood to be taken into account, for a start. When Akhenaten attempted to greatly extend the revival of the ancient cult of the sun god, and hence to remove the powerful influence of the Amun clergy at Karnak over the monarchy (see pages 43–44), he ran into resistance from the traditional religious authorities. Indeed, they eradicated his reforms immediately after his death. Then there were provincial governors *(nomarchs)*, who with other senior officials and administrators always sought to keep as much power in their own hands as possible; and of course the military commanders, all of whom were capable of acting in their own interests before turning to attend to the king. As a dispatch from an unruly general put it in the time of Rameses XI: "Pharaoh? Whose master is he these days?"

Sesostris III, who ruled from 1878 to 1841BC, was one of Egypt's most effective kings, radically reforming his adminstration and showing how authority could be successfully delegated. Other kings were less fortunate: despite the trappings of divinity, a number of pharaohs fell victim to political elements beyond their control.

The Dream of Tuthmosis

Between the paws of the Great Sphinx at Giza, one of the most powerful of all the monuments of Egypt, there lies a granite stele inscribed with a strange story – an account of certain curious events during the reign of King Amenhotep II (1427–1401BC).

Prince Tuthmosis overseeing workers who are clearing drifts of sand covering the body of the Great Sphinx of Giza.

It so happened, recounts the *stele*, that a young prince of the royal house was hunting in the desert near Giza. His name was Tuthmosis; and as one of the king's younger sons, he had no hopes of the succession – or so he believed.

That day the sun burned particularly fiercely, and by noon the prince was very weary. Finding himself close to the Great Sphinx – of which only the head still showed above the windblown desert sands – he sought out a cool

spot in its ancient shade and promptly fell asleep.

Immediately, there came upon him an extraordinary dream in which the Sphinx itself came to life and spoke to him, saying, "I am the sun god, and your father. Listen, and hear how you shall be the ruler of all Egypt." There was one condition – Tuthmosis must clear away the desert sands that were engulfing the Sphinx.

When he awoke, he hurried at once to Memphis to organize a team of workmen to shift the sand from the lion-body. The Sphinx remained true to its word and Tuthmosis was chosen as king above his elder brothers. In due course he was crowned as Tuthmosis IV. His reign lasted for ten years, and throughout that time he honoured the Sphinx.

royal permission to settle on the same land where they had fought, which happened to be one of the most fertile pieces of land in the region. Such indications that the enemy did not, perhaps, come off so badly after all had no place in royal myth.

A specific discrepancy between the official version of events and reality is found in the reign of Rameses II, a century earlier. Rameses II – "the Great" – spent many years struggling against the Hittite kingdom in Anatolia and northern Syria, at a time when Egypt controlled most of Palestine and the southern Lebanon. Between the two powers was a kind of political buffer zone.

In 1285BC, Rameses led a powerful expedition north through Gaza all the way to the Hittite city of Qadesh on the Orontes river. The advance guard of the Egyptian army, led by the king, had barely begun to make camp by Qadesh when the approaching support division was ambushed by a large force under the Hittite king Muwatallis. At least one Egyptian division was scattered; Rameses, commanding from the camp, managed to hold off the main Hittite attack long enough for reinforcements to arrive. The battle ended in some sort of stalemate, and a few days later the Egyptian host, or what was left of it, marched home again –

leaving Qadesh unscathed. From the Egyptian point of view, the battle was clearly a shambles from which they were lucky to escape without suffering total disaster.

For Rameses, though, it was a great victory, and he made sure that all Egypt knew of it. The battle is lavishly described on the walls of five of his temple buildings, at Abydos, Luxor, Karnak, Abu Simbel and the Ramesseum. And it was told and retold on endless papyri as an exercise for schoolboys and trainee scribes. In this "official" version, Rameses is surrounded by two and a half thousand Hittite chariots; yet with the aid of Amun – "Forward, I am with you/ I, your father, my hand is with you/ I prevail over a hundred thousand men" – the pharaoh sees the enemy off almost single-handed. After his mighty victory, the Hittites beg for peace. "Look, you spent yesterday killing a hundred thousand, and today you came back and left us no heirs. Be not hard in your dealings, victorious king! Peace is better than fighting. Give us breath." Rameses, marching briskly back to Egypt, is naturally prepared to be magnanimous.

A few years later, the Hittites were plagued by internal revolt and threatened from the east by Assyria. But the region was simply too far away for Egypt's domination to be long-lasting. In the end,

Rameses II, "the Great", shown with the creator god Amun. Rameses, on the left, wears the double crown of Upper and Lower Egypt, but there is little to distinguish the two figures – Rameses was himself a god, after all.

This image of Tuthmosis III radiates a tranquillity that belies his record as one of Egypt's most formidable military leaders. The Syrians took many years to recover from his campaigns.

with both sides weary of the constant destructive skirmishing, a treaty was signed in 1269BC between Rameses II and the new king of the Hittites, Hattusilis III.

This agreement – which has survived in both Egyptian and Hittite versions, each claiming that the first, humiliating request for peace came from the other – is the oldest existing example of a peaceable international accord. (A copy is kept in the United Nations building in New York.) The treaty seems to have been successful, since there were no further Hittite wars during the remainder of Rameses' sixty-six-year reign. As part of the settlement, in the thirty-third year of his reign, the pharaoh married a daughter of the Hittite king and, to consolidate matters still further, he married a second daughter eleven years later – events celebrated in temple and *stele* inscriptions.

A Cunning General

Even on those rare occasions when neither the pharaoh nor one of the other gods was the chief protagonist, every tale naturally redounded to the king's great credit. One of the more entertaining tales concerned the *ruse de guerre* used by Djehuty, a general of Tuthmosis III, to capture the city of Joppa (present-day Jaffa) in Canaan.

One account of this rebellion, written many years later, was, to a large extent, fictional. A revolt had taken place in Joppa, and not for the first time. During the course of his reign, Tuthmosis fought numerous campaigns in the area. Clearly, it was imperative to bring the city to heel at once. Tuthmosis, unable to leave Egypt, sent instead his resourceful General Djehuty, entrusting him with the royal mace as a sign of the powers that had been delegated to him.

When Djehuty reached Joppa, he was daunted by the city's towering walls. Reluctantly he ordered an all-out assault which resulted in heavy Egyptian losses, with nothing to show for them. So Djehuty decided to try cunning against his opponents. He sent a formal letter to the prince, once more demanding surrender. Attached

Sinuhe

One of Egypt's most-loved stories – it exists in many versions – celebrates the values that the pharaohs' subjects held dear. It tells the story of Sinuhe, a high court official of the Twelfth Dynasty.

Sinuhe was a trusted servant at the court of King Amenemhat. When his master died – it is thought by assassination – he was convinced that, regardless of his innocence, he might be implicated and punished by the king's successor. So he fled through the Sinai Desert, and sought refuge in Syria.

There he thrived mightily. The local prince showed him great favour, even granting him his eldest daughter in marriage. Over the years, he grew in

King Sesostris I is embraced by Ptah, creator-god of Memphis. Sesostris's father was apparently assassinated. The tale of the father's servant Sinuhe tells how he fled Egypt to escape suspicion of the murder.

wealth and stature. But all this was meaningless to Sinuhe, for there could be no real happiness for him outside his own country. At last Senwosert, who was now king, hearing of Sinuhe's unhappiness, sent a message to the former servant: "You shall not die abroad. Think of your dead body. Come home."

At once Sinuhe gave all his goods to his eldest son, and set off for Egypt. At last he met the king. "My limbs trembled," he said, "when this god addressed me." But Sesostris I was inclined to be generous: he made him a "Companion among the Nobles" and ordered that he should be bathed, anointed and dressed as an Egyptian once more.

Moreover, there was even better to come. For the king not only granted him land and a house – but, far more important to the Egyptians, he gave him a proper tomb.

to the official scroll, however, he added a private message: it was clear that he could not take the city, wrote the general, and he was much afraid of the consequent wrath of Tuthmosis. Therefore, for a handsome bribe, he would change sides. Perhaps the prince would agree to meet to discuss terms with him?

The prince, who ought to have known better, was willing to compromise. Under a flag of truce, the two men discussed matters amicably; then the prince asked if he could see the famous mace. In the privacy of Djehuty's tent, the general produced the great symbol of authority. But the prince did not have long to marvel at the mace before Djehuty knocked him unconscious, using the exquisite treasure as a weapon.

While some of his men bound the luckless ruler, Djehuty told the prince's servants that he had prepared many gifts for Joppa, to display where his new loyalties lay. The gifts were impressive and numerous: they filled two hundred large baskets, each carried by two unarmed men. The people of Joppa opened their gates to allow the tribute to enter.

Once inside, however, the trap was sprung. From each basket leapt an Egyptian soldier – with extra weapons for his two bearers. Within minutes, they had seized the gates, and the rest of Djehuty's men flooded through to victory.

In due course, the city's booty and its fettered prince were brought to Egypt and the king's ingenious general was heaped with rewards.

91

THE GREAT PYRAMIDS

Egypt has many astonishing edifices, but the greatest of them all is the colossal pyramid of King Khufu (known as Cheops by the Greeks) at Giza. The necropolis at Giza contains a number of Fourth Dynasty pyramids, all dominated by the sheer bulk of the Great Pyramid, originally called "the pyramid which is the place of sunrise and sunset". Standing more than one hundred and forty-six metres high, it is accompanied by the slightly smaller pyramid of Khephren (Khufu's son), and those of his son Menkaure and their queens' pyramids. Together these constructions make an unforgettable sight on the fringes of the modern city of Cairo.

Right: The portico of the tomb of the royal official Seshemnefer by the southeast corner of the Great Pyramid itself. Although the outer surfaces of the pyramids are uneven, they would have originally been covered by a smooth layer of white limestone, crowned in gold at the summit.

Figures carved in the limestone wall of an Old Kingdom tomb, near the stepped pyramid at Saqqara, 24 kilometres south of Giza. The nobles built their own tombs close to the royal burial sites in the hope that proximity to their king increased their chances of attaining immortality.

Above: The three pyramids at Giza were built (left to right) by Menkaure, his father Khephren and his grandfather Khufu. Khephren's complex was similar to that of Khufu but slightly smaller. Menkaure's pyramid underwent a series of changes and is probably incomplete.

Above: The Great Sphinx (see page 71), which has the body of a lion and the head of a man (in this case probably in the likeness of King Khephren), dominates the site at Giza. Situated alongside the causeway that leads to Khephren's pyramid, it measures twenty metres at the highest point.

Right: A map showing the main pyramid sites across ancient Egypt. The site at Giza is only one of many, albeit the grandest and best-preserved.

Abu Rawash ▲

Giza ▲

Zawyet-el-Aryan ▲

Abusir ▲

Saqqara ▲

Danshur ▲

Mazghuna ▲

el-Lisht ▲ *Nile*

Seila ▲   ▲ Maidum

Hawara ▲

▲ el-Lahun

THE THRONE OF OSIRIS

"Think of the day of your burial, your passing into a state of perfection ... A funeral procession will be made for you on the day of the entombment. The mummy case will be of gold, its head ornamented with lapis lazuli ... You will not die abroad!" These words, written by King Sesostris I around 1970BC, were addressed in a letter to Sinuhe, a former high official of the royal palace, who had chosen exile in Palestine. To a modern reader, this speech would hardly seem comforting, yet it reflected the primary ambition of most Egyptians: to be buried in the homeland after full preparation for the afterlife, so that their souls would live in Egypt for eternity.

Below: **The crocodile-headed monster, Ammut, whose body is half-lion, half-hippopotamus, stands with Thoth at the judgement of the dead.**

The ancient Egyptians were extremely conscious of their mortality. In an age when the average life-expectancy was around thirty-five years, it would have been foolish to regard death as too distant a prospect – even in the prime of life, it was necessary to make early arrangements for burial. For the elite, of course, preparation began years in advance with the building of the tomb. Any one of the pharaohs' pyramids would have taken several decades to construct.

The Egyptian royal tomb, which represented a monumental doorway to the afterlife, was usually built on the west bank of the Nile, where the sun god began his nightly descent into the underworld. The Old Kingdom *Pyramid Texts* describe the tradition of the dead king joining the sun god Re in his solar barque (see page 38). However, the tomb was more than just an entrance, the starting point of a journey: it was also a home. The dead Egyptian's mummified body and his vital force, known as the *ka*, were expected to live forever in the "house of eternity", or the "house of the *ka*". Moreover, the tomb had to contain the necessary funerary equipment and be inscribed with a variety of spells to protect the deceased from negative forces.

Opposite: **Osiris, lord of the underworld, tested the souls of the dead. He was frequently depicted on the walls of tombs, as in this painting (*c.*1145BC) from the Theban tomb of Kynebu, as a reminder to the soul of the judgement ahead. He is accompanied by the four sons of Horus whose heads were often depicted on Canopic jars.**

Even after elaborate physical preparations of the body had been completed, and the tomb had been prepared for the corpse, the soul still faced an arduous voyage through the underworld, where it had finally to prove itself before the throne of the god Osiris. If it completed the journey and was judged favourably by Osiris, the deceased would be transformed into one of the "blessed dead". But if the soul failed in Osiris's judgement, it was condemned to oblivion.

Preparing for Eternity

Ancient Egyptians believed that preserving the corpse was crucial to its attaining the afterlife. Initially, bodies buried in shallow pits were protected by the desiccating effect of the desert. Later, the process of mummification served the same function in the tomb.

In addition to the physical body (*sah*) and its heart (*ib*, regarded as the seat of intelligence and emotion), the Egyptians believed that each individual was made up of five distinctive parts: the *ka* (life-force or soul), the *ba* (personality or spirit), the *akh* (immortal unification of the *ka* and *ba*), the *ren* (name) and the *shuwt* (shadow). Both the name and the shadow had metaphysical qualities thought to protect the individual. This fivefold division had particular significance after death, during the hazardous journey through the underworld.

When the creator god Khnum moulded every person from clay at birth, he created a spiritual replica, called the *ka*. After death the *ka* was free to dwell in the tomb, absorbing the life-giving

Two mummies at the end of the 70-day mummification process, from a fragment of a painted wall scene from the 18th-Dynasty Theban tomb of Meryma'at, priest of Ma'at (1391–1353BC). The body had to be preserved in the best form possible in readiness for the pleasures of the hereafter.

properties of the offerings (known as *kaw*) left by priests and the family. The *ba*, similar to our concept of the personality, was usually shown as a human-headed bird that dwelt in the tomb at night. Its distinctive physical qualities differentiated one individual from another. The *ba* could also represent a god's power on earth: the Memphite Apis bull, for example, was the *ba* of Osiris (see page 68). Unlike the *ka*, the *ba* was able to visit the living world or travel through the heavens with the gods. Its role in guaranteeing the deceased's immortality was crucial: it had to travel through the underworld, overcoming a series of trials, before it could be reunited with the *ka* and become an *akh*.

The *akh*, symbolized by a crested ibis, represented the final and most complete form of existence to which every Egyptian aspired, and once formed would last for eternity. In some funerary texts it is written that the *akh* dwelt in the heavens with the gods. But the formation of the *akh*, which resulted from the unification of the *ka* and *ba*, depended on the successful physical preparation of the corpse for the afterlife. The Egyptians believed that life after death could be enjoyed only if three conditions were met: the dead body had to be preserved in pristine condition; the *ka* had to be supplied with sustenance; and the deceased's name had to be commemorated by prayer.

Mummification

The first step towards meeting these conditions was to initiate a process, now known as mummification, designed to preserve the corpse. This involved evisceration (removal of the internal organs), followed by dehydration of the body with natron – a form of sodium that absorbed water.

Anubis, God of Mummification

Anubis was the protective deity of cemeteries, credited with the invention of embalming because he helped Isis to preserve her brother Osiris, whose body was the first to be mummified. Usually depicted as a reclining black jackal, or a man with a jackal head, he was thought to ward off scavengers. Osiris's blackness symbolized the rich soil of Egypt and the appearance of a mummified corpse.

The jackal-headed god Anubis attends to a dead person in his role as an embalmer. This 19th-Dynasty wall painting is from the tomb of the workman Sennedjem at Deir el-Medina in Thebes.

Mummification was a complex procedure which involved a series of detailed operations and rituals.

To begin with, the body was washed and purified, and then the perishable organs were removed. First, the brain was extracted through the nasal passage using a long metal hook, and then the left side of the body was opened up to remove the liver, lungs, stomach and intestines. The brains were discarded as worthless, but the heart, which was seen as the seat of all thought, was left in place. The removed organs were then washed and dried separately with natron (a type of sodium salt), treated with aromatic oils and resins, wrapped in linen, and then placed into the four Canopic jars – so-called because of a long-standing misconception that they were related to human-headed jars that were worshipped as manifestations of Osiris in the Delta port of Canopus.

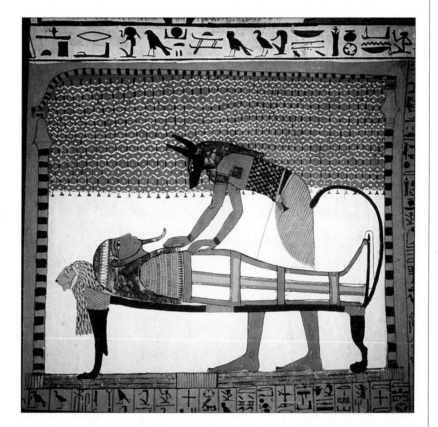

Each jar was then entrusted to the care of one of Horus's four sons, who were believed to be present at the soul's final judgement before Osiris. The liver was protected by the human-headed Imsety, the lungs by the baboon-headed Hapy, the stomach by the jackal-headed Duamutef, and the intestines by the hawk-headed Qebehsenuef. Each creature featured on the stoppers of the jars.

After evisceration the body cavity was washed out and scented, then stuffed with temporary packing which included natron to help dry the body's interior. Natron was also placed over the corpse for forty days. During this stage in the process, the body lost up to seventy-five per cent of its weight. The temporary stuffing would even be removed and the body cavity refilled with fresh natron and resin-soaked linen to restore its former shape, after which cosmetic decorations were made. After being coated in cedar oil and scented resins, the body was wrapped in bandages while priests read out the appropriate incantations from *The Book of the Dead.*

The corpse was then anointed with aromatic oils and resin before being wrapped in strips of linen. The oldest intact mummy found *in situ* was discovered in the Saqqara tomb of a court singer, Nefer, who died *c.*2470BC. He was expertly wrapped and preserved, with details such as eyebrows and a moustache painted onto his bandaged face.

As the embalmers acquired experience, certain techniques gained prestige and the experts codified their practices in manuals that described each step of the work. The oldest such manuals date from the first century AD, but they are undoubtedly based on earlier texts. Initially mummification was reserved for royalty, but gradually embalming became available to all who could afford it. By the time of Herodotus, in the fifth century BC, it had become a relatively common phenomenon. The Greek historian described a scene in an embalming parlour:

Many mummified bodies have been found in a remarkable state of preservation some thousands of years after death. One such is this head of an unknown person.

"When a corpse is carried in to [the embalmers], they show the bearers wooden models of mummies, painted in exact imitation of the real thing. The best method of embalming, so they say, is that which was practised on [the god Osiris]. The second method that they demonstrate is rather inferior and costs less. The third is cheapest of all. Having indicated the differences, they ask by which method the corpse is to be prepared. And when the bearers have agreed a price and departed, the embalmers, left behind in the workshop, set to work."

Despite such commercialism, embalming continued to hold mystic significance. Regardless of cost, the minimum length of time required to complete a mummification was seventy days. This period was not determined by practicalities: experiments have shown that the procedure had no benefit beyond forty days. There is biblical evidence in *Genesis* that Jacob was embalmed, probably because his son Joseph was a high official at the Egyptian court and because Jacob's body had to be returned to Canaan for burial. "Forty days were fulfilled for him, for so are fulfilled the days of those which are embalmed; and the Egyptians mourned for him for three score and ten days." The Egyptians clearly mourned until the seventy-day period was complete. The length of time necessary to mummify the corpse may have been dictated by the period when the rising Dog Star, Sirius, was temporarily hidden by its proximity to the sun. Sirius was of particular importance because its appearance heralded the annual flood.

The Ripper-out

In the most elaborate embalming rituals, the body was subjected to rather more complicated procedures. For example, although it was possible to remove some internal organs via bodily orifices without making an incision, it was easier to open up the abdominal cavity. This operation was performed with a flint blade by the "ripper-out" or "slitter", as the Greeks graphically called the

Amulets were often distributed among the bandages of a mummy to protect it during its voyage through the underworld. This glazed scarab amulet, *c.*1295BC, depicts the sun god in his morning form as Khepri, flanked by the sisters Isis and Nepthys.

practitioner. According to Greek sources, he was then ritually chased from the corpse – an act that possibly alluded to the role of Seth in the Osiris myth (see pages 75–84).

Protecting the Dead

The Egyptians' meticulous treatment of the body after death corresponded to their concern for the spirit, which also required a great deal of preparation before embarking on its journey through the underworld. During this voyage the *ba* was expected to encounter a variety of hazards, and so the living equipped the dead with many magical devices, such as protective amulets which were placed in the bandages surrounding the corpse. One of particular importance was the so-called *djed* pillar, an upright column topped by four cross-bars. Its origin remains uncertain, but *The Book of the Dead* refers to it as the backbone of Osiris, and it was intended to give the corpse stability in the afterlife. At various sites in Egypt the

ceremony of "The Raising of the Djed Pillar" was performed during royal jubilee festivals and during rituals for the dead king.

There were other types of amulet, including the heart scarab, which alludes to the heart's role as the seat of all intelligence and the centre of personality. As such, the heart would be weighed during the judgement before Osiris, and, if it was found to be heavy with sin, the deceased would be condemned. To prevent the heart from confessing its sin, the heart scarab was placed over the chest among the mummy wrappings, and inscribed with Chapter 30 of *The Book of the Dead*: "Oh my heart which I had from my mother, Oh my heart which I had upon earth, do not rise up against me as a witness in the presence of the Lord of Things." Additional amulets could be shaped as miniature gods and goddesses or parts of the body. The former were protective, while the latter acted as substitutes if, by misfortune, the embalming process should fail. Thus arrayed, and wrapped within its outer shroud, the body was ready for the coffin.

Coffins and Tombs

Laying the corpse to rest was accompanied by rituals no less elaborate than those of mummification. Around the time of the unification of the Two Lands (3100BC), coffins were generally made of mud, basketwork or wood, with the body (not embalmed at this period) doubled-up inside. Later the mummified corpse was usually laid out flat inside one or more wooden coffins, one within the other, both covered in spells and texts to assist the deceased in the afterlife. Sometimes the coffins were fashioned in human form, and were painted to resemble the deceased occupant and inscribed with further protective texts. The wealthy could also afford an extra layer, consisting of a stone sarcophagus (from a Greek word meaning "flesh-eating") within which the wooden coffins would be carefully placed.

Tombs can be seen as larger versions of coffins. The walls were painted with scenes of daily life alongside visions of the afterlife, spells to protect the deceased, and symbols of rebirth. Also contained within the tomb walls were funerary papyri, such as *The Book of the Dead* (see page 26), *The Book of Gates* and *The Book of Caverns,* which were also placed in the tomb to help the *ba* overcome the many difficulties ahead.

Inside the tomb was everything that the dead person might need: furniture, clothing, food, tools, boats (for the journey) and sometimes even toilet facilities. Also among the grave goods were personal items that the deceased had used or had been fond of when alive. Another important inclusion in the tomb was a statue or image of the departed. It was believed that the *ka* could inhabit this representation in order to enjoy the items

The Opening of the Mouth

This crucial tombside ceremony was designed to revitalize the deceased by restoring his or her senses so that the body could become animated once again in readiness for the afterlife.

The ceremony appears to derive from a rite originally performed on gods' statues so that they could partake in ritual. The Old Kingdom *Pyramid Texts* refer to the mummy of the king as being involved in a re-enactment of Horus restoring the body of his father Osiris. By the New Kingdom the ceremony was performed (with many different stages) at every funeral. The coffin was placed in front of the tomb and was then purified with water and incense. Different parts of the body were restored to life with incantations and ceremonial implements, including the *peshkef* knife, an iron *netjeri* blade and an adze. Then the right foreleg of a sacrificial ox was held to the deceased's mouth, possibly to transfer the animal's symbolic power to the corpse. Occasionally, the ceremony was performed not on the body but on its tomb statue, which was believed to be inhabited by the *ka*.

As described in *The Book of the Dead*, the Opening of the Mouth ceremony was performed with ritual instruments on the mummy, which was held up by a priest wearing the mask of Anubis, guardian of the necropolis.

left for it, and such a figure could also act as a substitute for the body if the mummy was destroyed. In Old Kingdom *mastaba* tombs, such statues were often placed inside buildings which today we call *serdabs* (the ancient term was *per tuwt*, meaning "statue house"). These were small rooms with holes at eye-level through which the *ka* of the deceased could see and magically absorb the beneficial offerings and observe the commemorative rituals performed on its behalf. Sometimes a stone portrait head (now known as a "reserve head") was also placed in the tomb.

The final earthly stage on the journey to eternity was the funeral itself. In a procession accompanied by a crowd of professional mourners, who pulled at their hair and smeared their faces with dust in traditional gestures of grief, the mummified body was taken to the tomb, with family, friends and servants carrying funerary goods and the deceased's belongings. The funeral was also attended by the embalmer and the funerary priests, and when the procession arrived at the tomb it was greeted by *muu* dancers in distinctive reed headdresses. If a pharaoh was being buried, it is likely that most of Egypt's populace turned out to mark the event.

The climax of the funeral came with a ceremony called "The Opening of the Mouth", in which the deceased's *ka* was re-animated by the funerary priest (see opposite). Then priests and retinue departed, leaving workers to fill the tomb entrance with rubble and coat it in plaster. The plaster on a king's tomb was impressed with an image of a recumbent jackal representing Anubis, guardian of the necropolis and god of embalming.

In basing their view of the afterlife so strongly on material considerations such as the condition of the corpse, the sustenance of the *ka* and the continuation of priestly rituals, the Egyptians left their spirits open to all the dangers of mortal existence. The scavenging jackal was one of these perils (as one later Egyptologist remarked, he only needed to follow jackal trails to find a grave). But while it was comparatively easy to protect the corpse against jackals, human scavengers constituted a

Rock-cut tombs near Qena in Upper Egypt. In order to protect a body from tomb-robbers, the entrance to a rock-cut tomb was often carefully concealed.

greater threat. Throughout Egypt's history grave-robbing was rife. Despite all precautions, most graves were ransacked. In the Valley of the Kings on the west bank of the Nile, a practice was adopted of separating the tombs from the mortuary temples where priests conducted daily ceremonies ensuring the deceased's well-being in the afterlife. In this way, funerary rituals could take place without drawing attention to the whereabouts of the body. Nevertheless, a mortuary temple indicated that a tomb was in the vicinity, and mummies and funerary treasures were still violated. Even after the separation of the tomb from the temple site, the Valley of the Kings was patrolled by guards. But the pharaohs' graves were never entirely impenetrable – any disruption in political stability gave tomb-robbers ample opportunity to forcefully enter the burial chambers and pillage the funerary goods.

101

Journey into Darkness

When the spirit left the body, it was thought to wander the pathways and corridors of the underworld in search of the Hall of Judgement where Osiris sat on his throne. Throughout the journey, the soul used spells to overcome hostile beings such as serpents and demons.

After death, the Egyptians hoped to become one with Osiris, god of resurrection and the under-world. Through him alone could immortality be achieved. He was usually shown wrapped as a mummy clutching the emblems of kingship, the crook and flail, which indicated his original role as an earthly ruler and father of Horus, with whom all pharaohs were identified (see page 75). Known as the "eternally incorruptible", he additionally acquired the epithet "foremost of the Westerners", a description originally applied to his predecessor as god of the dead, the jackal god Khentimentiu. First mentioned in the Fifth Dynasty (*c*.2350BC),

This painted scene from inside the tomb of King Rameses I (1307–1306BC) shows Re, in his ram-headed form as "Flesh of Re", on his journey through the *Duat* in the Boat of Millions. The deceased pharaoh was believed to join Re on this voyage. Other tomb paintings of this subject show the boat filled with crowds of figures believed to be the souls of the blessed.

Osiris was an important figure in the mythological tradition based in the cult centre of Heliopolis where Re was principal deity. There may have been rivalry between the two gods, who were both key figures in the underworld. However, a description of the couple embracing to become

Osiris, Lord of the Underworld

Osiris's main function was to rule the underworld, but he also acted as a god of fertility and agriculture. One of the most enduring deities, he was worshipped throughout Egypt as patron of the dead, lord of the necropolis and the guarantor of rebirth.

Osiris was of prime importance in Egyptian mythology. As a god of fertility, he was seen as the life force behind all things.

Yet, at the same time, he was lord of the underworld, and this combination of aspects led him to be identified with resurrection. Osiris was reborn after he had been killed by Seth, who dismembered his body and scattered it across Egypt (see page 76). His resurrection was achieved with the help of his sister Isis, who reassembled his scattered limbs in the form of the first mummy so that his spirit could inhabit his body once again.

Osiris's main cult centre was Abydos, in Upper Egypt, where his head was thought to be interred. Some priests went so far as to claim that the tomb of the First Dynasty monarch Djer, who ruled around 2900BC, was in fact Osiris's burial place. But the god was also described as "he who dwells in Heliopolis", which was the cult centre of Re, thereby linking him with the sun god.

This statue of Osiris from the 26th Dynasty (c.664–525BC) shows his crown typically flanked by ostrich feathers and adorned with the *uraeus* (cobra) which symbolized the power of kingship. He also holds in his hands the crook and flail, two further insignia of sovereignty.

"Twin Souls" would suggest that this opposition was in due course resolved.

Osiris's role in mythology was complex: strongly associated with the living earth, he was also identified with death. So important was the union between the individual soul and Osiris that in funerary inscriptions the god's name became a prefix of the deceased's own name – thus X, when alive, became Osiris-X after death. Osiris was considered an equitable god, and it was thought that all who had been virtuous in life would be granted entry by him to the afterlife. But even the most virtuous conscience had to prove itself: while the body lay in the tomb, its *ba* had to undergo a series of arduous tests before achieving its ultimate aim – spiritual bliss in the hereafter.

The Duat

The Egyptians' vision of the afterlife was modelled on the land of the living. There was a river with sandy shores – directly analogous to the Nile –

which ran through a plain surrounded on all sides by mountains. A narrow gorge at the western end, through which the sun god entered at the end of the day and humans passed at the end of their lives, was the only feature that could not be found on earth.

As a replica of Egypt, this underworld domain was in many ways familiar to every Egyptian, but for the newly-arrived *ba* it held terrifying obstacles. The topography of the *Duat* included natural features such as lakes, deserts and islands but it also held hazards such as lakes of fire and a mound from which a head, called the flesh of Isis, emerged as the soul approached. The *ba's* way was also hindered by demons, with names such as "Backward-facing one who comes from the abyss". They tried to ensnare the *ba* with sticks, spears, bird-traps and nets, and the soul could protect itself only if it had knowledge of the demons' secret names. Funerary texts supplied maps of the underworld, together with all the spells necessary to overcome the hazards encountered there. These texts also described the fates lying in wait for those who were judged to be the enemies of Re – beheading, dismemberment, sacrificial burning or being boiled alive in a cauldron.

Like the sun god Re on his nightly voyage, the *ba* passed through the *Duat* until the moment

The jackal-headed god Anubis was responsible for weighing the heart of the deceased against the feather of truth, belonging to Ma'at (top right). The Devourer of the Condemned Dead waits hungrily for those hearts that are heavy with sin. This image is commonly found in *Book of the Dead* funerary scenes.

of rebirth finally arrived. Unlike Re, however, who negotiated all twelve hours of the night, the *ba* had to go no further than the Sixth Hour to discover its destiny. Here Osiris sat on his throne in the hall of judgement flanked by the goddesses Isis and Nephthys. Before him, the heart of the deceased was weighed on scales against the feather of Ma'at, goddess of Truth, Divine Order and Justice. The scales were then checked by Anubis and the result recorded by Thoth. At the same time, the deceased declared that he or she was innocent of specific crimes, in a ritual called the "Negative Confession". These offences included treason, boastfulness and deceit, but mostly were of a civic nature, including crimes against the laws of property. The *ba* had to stand before a tribunal of forty-two assessor gods, and address each one by name. The Negative Confession provided the *ba* with total immunity: "nothing evil shall come into being against me ... in this Hall of Justice because I know the names of these gods who are in it".

If the balance of Osiris's scales should tip towards the heart, then the soul was heavy with sin and redemption was lost; if it should tip the other way, the soul was saved. Lurking ravenously beneath the scales was the monster Ammut, "Devourer of the Condemned Dead", who had the head of a dog or a crocodile, the forelegs of a lion and the hindquarters of a hippopotamus. Into the jaws of this monster the heart of the deceased was destined to fall if it was encumbered with wrongdoing.

Magic Texts

Various texts inside the tomb proffered spells and other safeguards to protect the deceased's soul against an unfavourable judgement and malevolent spirits in the *Duat*. Particularly effective were those spells inscribed on heart scarab amulets, which were believed to prevent the heart from testifying against its owner (see page 99). Similar safeguards could be found in the *Coffin Texts*, which contained advice on "How not to rot and not to do work in the kingdom of the dead."

Although the funerary texts were often quite precise in their directions for attaining immortality, they also presented more than one view of the soul's destination. In some interpretations the soul rose to the sky, although the texts differed on the exact destination. The Old Kingdom *Pyramid Texts*

placed the dead pharaoh among the circumpolar stars (that is, stars that turn in a circle around the North Pole), as well as describing him joining Re's entourage in the solar barque. Ultimately, they identified the dead king with Osiris himself. During the Middle Kingdom these divergent funerary beliefs became more widespread through the *Coffin Texts*. One of these, known as *The Book of Two Ways*, complicated the picture further by allocating a place for the spirit in the night sky among the attendants of Thoth, the moon god. This source also provided a map, with two alternative paths (possibly one of fire and one of water) to assist the deceased on his or her journey to the lands of Osiris. The idea of spending an eternity with Osiris, in his role as god of resurrection,

The soul of the dead had to undergo various trials and tests in the underworld. This priest from the 21st Dynasty (1070–945BC) is threatened by three demons who are armed with knives. The bound ass above the demons represents one of their previous victims, turned into animal form.

Servants of the Dead

In the earliest times pharaonic tombs were surrounded by pits containing the bodies of servants who were expected to serve their master in death as in life. Human attendants were later replaced by models, often inscribed with hieroglyphs.

Just as the pharaoh might ask his subjects to perform various labours, so might the gods ask the spirit of the deceased to work on their behalf. To avoid an afterlife of eternal servitude, Egyptians were buried with models representing attendants who would do physical work for them. Called *shabtis*, after the Egyptian word *wesheb* meaning "answer", these little figurines were expected to answer whatever demands were made on the soul with an eager "Here I am! I shall do it!"

Up to four hundred and one *shabtis* could be buried in a tomb. This number included a servant for every day of the year, and thirty-six foremen to organize each group of ten workers. The *shabtis* were generally inscribed with the name of their owner and the sixth chapter of *The Book of the Dead*, which enabled the figures to accomplish their tasks. One surviving text refers to a noblewoman who actually paid the *shabtis* in advance. This action bound the *shabtis* contractually to her, and ensured that she herself would not have to work for the gods in the afterlife.

The use of these figurines began during the Middle Kingdom, and developed from the Old Kingdom use of funerary statues. It was not until the Ptolemaic period that *shabtis* ceased to be popular.

This *shabti* and its model sarcophagus represented Huy, a royal steward and scribe of Amenhotep III. Only 14cm high, he is shown holding amulets symbolizing *sa* (protection) and *djed* (stability).

became increasingly popular, and developed into the New Kingdom texts that we now call *The Book of the Dead*.

In the earliest of the *Pyramid Texts*, the deceased pharaoh was described as crossing to the eastern part of the sky to join the sun god: "The sky's reed floats are launched for Unas [the particular pharaoh to whom this text refers], that he may cross on them to light-land, to Re." To make this crossing, the deceased pharaoh had to summon the Ferryman, called "Backwards Looker" because of the direction he faced during the passage: "Awake in peace, Backwards Looker ... Unas has come to you that you might ferry him in this boat in which you ferry the gods." However, the Ferryman would only accept his royal passenger on the two conditions that he could show himself to be free of sin, and that he could say the Ferryman's name and the names of each part of his boat – once again, the Egyptians' obsession with naming came to the fore.

On the far shore of what seems to have been envisaged as a vast celestial lake, heralds greeted the pharaoh and announced his arrival to the other gods. In a gesture of welcome and goodwill, accepting him as one of their own, the gods "cast off their white sandals to earth ... They throw off their garments. 'Our heart was not glad until thy coming,' they say."

Although some texts described the pharaoh in the afterlife as ruling a court, as he had done on

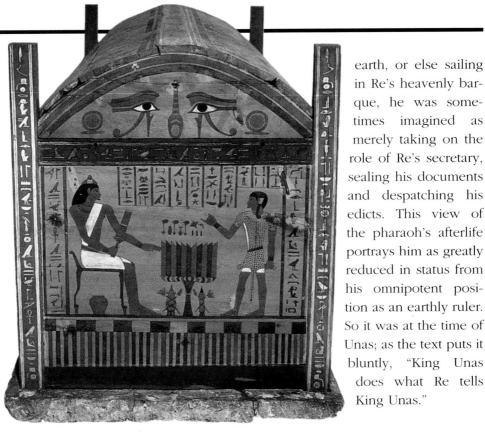

Beliefs as to the destiny of virtuous souls varied. This coffin from Thebes (*c.*650BC) shows the deceased seated opposite a priest. Between the two figures are some loaves shaped to allude to the Field of Reeds, where the dead enjoyed the afterlife in a land of fecundity.

earth, or else sailing in Re's heavenly barque, he was sometimes imagined as merely taking on the role of Re's secretary, sealing his documents and despatching his edicts. This view of the pharaoh's afterlife portrays him as greatly reduced in status from his omnipotent position as an earthly ruler. So it was at the time of Unas; as the text puts it bluntly, "King Unas does what Re tells King Unas."

The Field of Reeds

In one portrayal of the afterlife, the deceased inhabited an underworld that corresponded to Egypt. This region, known in some texts as the Field of Reeds, lay below the western horizon, and was presided over by Osiris. Occasionally, it was represented as a string of islands that were reached by a magical boat. Here the fortunate dead could enjoy a world of astonishing fertility, and resume human activities such as eating, drinking and lovemaking, as promised in the *Coffin Texts*. However, as in life on earth, these recreations could not be savoured until after the crops had been harvested and construction work completed. To release them from these chores, the dead were equipped with spells and diminutive model servants, packed among their grave goods, who would answer any call made on them (see opposite).

At the same time there was a more spiritual view of the afterlife, involving Osiris in his role as god of fertility. In this version, the soul was

Egyptian tombs were filled with reminders of the gods and of
the spirit of the deceased, but that did not prevent robbers
from risking fatal curses in order to ransack them.
This tomb, of a certain Pashedu at Deir el-Medina,
was almost certainly raided for its treasures.

mosquito bite in April 1923, six weeks after opening the burial chamber. The press capitalized on the coincidence, and before long any mishap connected either with Carnarvon or the tomb was being hailed as a result of the curse. As it happened, there were plenty of mishaps to report.

That September Carnarvon's younger brother died unexpectedly. Then an X-ray specialist called in to examine the mummy died *en route*. An American financier fell victim of pneumonia after visiting the tomb. A French Egyptologist had a fatal fall following a similar visit. Richard Bethell, a member of Carnarvon's team, died in mysterious circumstances and Bethell's father comitted suicide

shortly afterwards. To add to the tragedy, a child of eight was accidentally killed by the hearse.

The rumour mill worked overtime. The reality, though, was less sensational. A decade later, of the twenty-six people present at the tomb's opening, only six had died. Of the twenty-two who had witnessed the opening of the sarcophagus, two had died. None of those who had watched the mummy being unwrapped was a victim. In fact, one of the first to enter the tomb, Lord Carnarvon's daughter, died aged seventy-nine, and the man who autopsied the mummy lived longer still. If Tutankhamun's spirit had indeed returned in anger, its vengeance was peculiarly selective.

Setne Khamwas and the Book of Magic

The dangers of interfering with the dead are highlighted by the story of Setne Khamwas. Based on the historical figure of Khamwas, a high priest of Ptah and the fourth son of Rameses II, the tale was discovered on papyri dating from the third century BC.

The scholar Setne Khamwas plays draughts to win possession of Thoth's book of magic.

Setne Khamwas, a learned scholar, was intrigued to hear about a book of magic that had been written by the god Thoth. This book, he was assured, was hidden in the tomb of Prince Neferkaptah in the vast necropolis to the west of Memphis. Setne Khamwas determined at once that the book should be his.

He found the tomb and, with the help of his brother Inaros, forced it open. There, shining brightly, was the magic book, but when Setne Khamwas reached to take it, he was confronted by the spirits of the dead prince Neferkaptah, his wife Ihwey, and their son Merib.

Setne Khamwas tried to snatch the book from Neferkaptah, who stopped him. "If you want the book," he said, "you will have to play draughts for it." They took out a board and began to play.

Setne Khamwas lost three games. After each victory, Neferkaptah hit his opponent over the head and drove him into the ground until, finally, only his head was above the soil. At this point Setne Khamwas sent his brother to fetch his magic amulets and, by their power, he was able to break free and grab the book.

On his return to the outside world, he began to read avidly, ignoring all advice to return the book. Shortly afterwards, however, he saw a beautiful woman walking past his window and was smitten with desire. He begged her to make love to him. She said she would, but only on condition that he hand all his property over to her and kill his own children. Setne Khamwas agreed, little knowing that the woman was a spirit called Tabubu and that he was under her spell.

Setne Khamwas had hardly had time to remove his clothes when Tabubu vanished, and the pharaoh entered the room. His embarrassment was relieved only by the news that it had all been a bad dream and his children were still alive. He determined to return the book to Neferkaptah's grave and relinquish ownership of it.

The dead prince greeted him with amusement but demanded a favour to atone for the theft. His request was that Setne Khamwas find the bodies of his wife and son and bring them to him. Setne Khamwas unearthed the bodies and returned them to Neferkaptah's tomb, which he then sealed, consigning the dangerous book to eternity.

tomb of the little-known boy-king, whose reign (1333–1323BC) lasted only ten years. Brimming with funerary equipment made from the finest materials, the small chamber was also decorated with depictions of the afterlife.

Above: Queen Ankhesenamun assists the young king during a royal bird hunt. From a panel on the right-hand side of a small gilded shrine, this tender scene evokes aspects of the couple's life together.

Left: Lions were revered by the Egyptians and deified as Bastet and Re (see pages 66–67). This protective lioness-head, made of gilded wood with eye markings of blue glass, is part of a funerary couch – one of three ritual couches found in the antechamber of Tutankhamun's tomb.

Above: The lavishly decorated golden mask of Tutankhamun is generally recognized as the greatest of Egypt's ancient treasures. It covered the head of the mummified pharaoh. Spell 151b from *The Book of the Dead*, engraved on the back of the mask, gave it an important protective function.

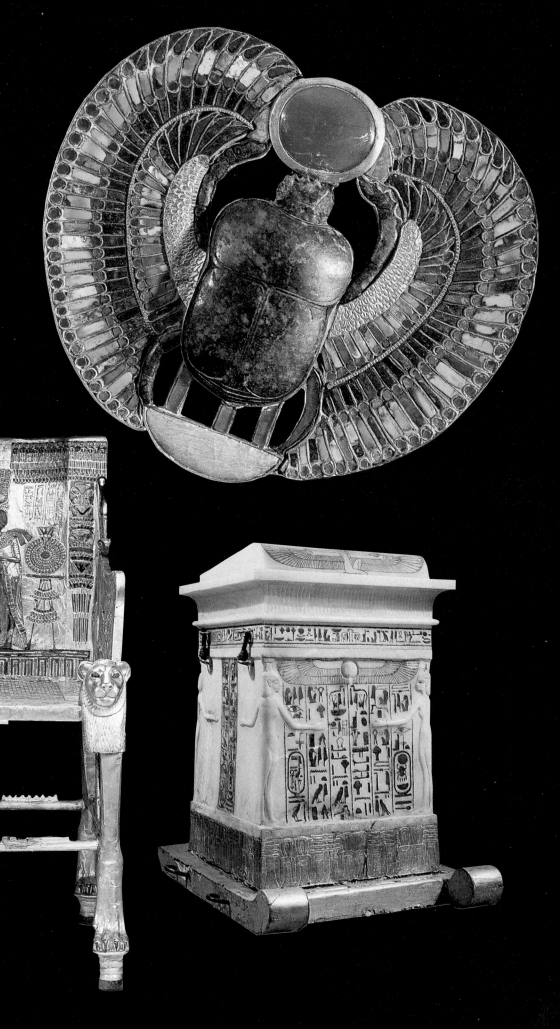

Right: The scarab beetle represented the sun god Re. This exquisite pectoral ornament, found in a jewel box in the tomb, bears signs that include the king's throne name.

Below left: The feet of Tutankhamun's throne take the form of lion claws and lion heads surmount its front legs to symbolize power. The backrest displays a royal scene beneath the sun disc.

Below right: This beautiful two-metre-high canopic chest was carved from a single block of calcite (quartz). The goddesses Isis, Nephthys, Selkis and Neith embrace the four corners of the shrine. Beneath its lid are funerary jars.

TALES OF MAGIC AND FANTASY

"Egypt", declared Clement of Alexandria in the third century AD, "is the mother of magicians." As a leader of the early Church, pious Clement did not approve of a culture that championed spells and enchantment; but the truth of his statement would not have been doubted. By the Graeco-Roman period, Egypt was regarded throughout the classical world as the home of magic, and many Greek scholars visited the country to further their own learning.

Indeed, magic suffused the spiritual life of Egypt's people much as the Nile's annual deposit of rich silt fertilized their soil and nourished the crops that sustained them. It was perceived as a divine creative force (known as *heka*) that had existed since the beginning of time, and even before: *heka* furnished the power used by the first gods to bring the world into being.

Heka was often described as "the art of the mouth", as it depended on incantation and spells. The written word was thought to be even more powerful. Thus the greatest magicians in Egypt were the *hery-heb*, or "lector priests", who were responsible for the sacred temple papyri. They spent their lives immersed in magic and were known to have the power of *heka* in their voices: their ability to utter fatal curses, for example, put lesser mortals in awe of them.

Just as it informed and animated religion, *heka* was also an integral part of Egyptian science and technology. Physicians and other educated men were expected to know the rudiments of magic. A doctor not versed in its use would be regarded as less adept in treating a patient.

As magic and religion were inseparably intertwined, *heka* was essentially a godly power. However, knowledge of magic was not something that could be learned, but was blessing bestowed or withheld. People so blessed were known as the *hekau*, and the greatest among these were the pharaohs, who qualified on account of the divine origins of kingship.

Magic ritual guided Egyptians through all the stages of their lives, from birth into old age. It could protect them against disaster and disease; and if, for some reason, it failed, victims still had the comfort of knowing that every possible magical remedy had been tried on their behalf.

The goddess Isis, whether portrayed as a self-possessed woman (*above*) or an icon encumbered by her regalia (*opposite*), was venerated by all Egyptians as "great in magic".

Practitioners of Magic

Magicians often featured as the heroes of Egyptian myth, defying disease and performing miracles. Kings and quarrymen, doctors and diplomats, midwives and mariners: all relied on at least a little magic to help them get through life. Magical powers were accessible to priests, healers and scorpion-charmers, and everyone deferred to Egypt's gods, who were the greatest magicians of all.

Isis is often shown, as in this Late Period BC sculpture, suckling her infant son Horus. Venerated for her healing powers, this goddess was also Egypt's archetypal wife and mother.

The Egyptian pantheon was steeped in magic. It conditioned the atmosphere in which the gods evolved; it was the medium through which they disbursed their power, the armament with which they fought their quarrels. But no deity possessed such mastery of the art as the goddess Isis, whom most Egyptians believed to be the most powerful magician in the universe.

Isis had proved her mastery of magic at the beginning of time, when she used it to restore the dismembered body of her husband Osiris, the ruler, protector and judge of the dead (see pages 76–84). This story of resurrection was recorded in funerary inscriptions (known as the *Pyramid Texts*; see page 26) dating from the middle of the third millennium BC, but incorporating even older tales and spells.

One of Isis's most important skills was her ability to heal the sick. A surviving text includes a spell to cure burns and fevers which works by a symbolic change of identity. For the spell's duration, the patient becomes Horus, the son of Isis. The goddess then enters the patient's room to ask for water. When told that there is none available, she replies: "Water is within my mouth and a Nile flood between my thighs." Isis then cures the patient by using her own magical body fluids, saliva and urine. This spell had to be recited over a concoction of gum and cat hairs mixed with the milk of a woman who had given birth to a boy; the mixture was then smeared over the patient so as to make the fever abate.

Although Isis's magical powers were fabled from at least the second millennium BC, and her

Isis and the Seven Scorpions

Having murdered Osiris, the husband and brother of Isis, their evil brother Seth kept the goddess and her young son Horus as hostages. One night the captives broke free with the aid of the god Thoth, who provided an escort of seven scorpions to assist them in their daring escape.

Isis, with Horus and the scorpions in tow, came upon a village, in need of food and shelter. The first house that she tried belonged to a wealthy noblewoman who promptly slammed the door in the face of the entire party. Isis continued unshaken, and soon found the dilapidated home of a poor peasant girl who was only too happy to offer the goddess hospitality.

The scorpions, however, were enraged by the rich woman's brusque treatment of the goddess and her son, and so they prepared to avenge their mistress. Six of them passed their venom into the tail of the seventh, who crept into the noblewoman's house and stung

After the death of her husband and brother Osiris, Isis was protected by Thoth's seven scorpions.

her young son. As the boy lay dying, his mother ran around the town crying for help; but in payment for her earlier inhospitality, no one came to her aid.

Isis, however, took pity on the young boy, whom she felt should not be punished on his mother's account, and so she cast a powerful spell over him. By reciting the names of the seven scorpions, she neutralized the poison, so that the child recovered at once. His mother, truly repentant, gave all her belongings to Isis and the poor peasant girl.

This story was incorporated into one of the most potent spells to give protection against venomous stings.

role as a goddess of healing was celebrated long before that, it was not until late in Egypt's history that she became a prominent cult figure, with temples dedicated to her alone.

By the Ptolemaic period, however, Isis was thought to protect more than just the sick, and her powers were revered across Egypt. Her greatest temple was built around 380BC at Philae, on an island in the Nile close to the Nubian border (see page 127). There, the goddess was considered "more powerful than a thousand soldiers" and it was believed that she sheltered Egypt from invasion. This protective force also nullified the powers of Nubian sorcerers who frequently appear in Egyptian tales as dangerous and formidable adversaries. Who better than Isis, the universal mother and nurturer, to shield her people from alien harm?

Thoth, God of Knowledge

Of the male gods, the mightiest in magic was the moon god Thoth, who was either represented as a human figure with the head of an ibis or as a baboon. Revered as the god of knowledge and writing, he was often shown carrying the scribal tools of ink palette and pen which he used to record all things. Because written magic was believed so powerful, Thoth, as the inventor of hieroglyphs, was also held to be the inventor of magic itself.

Since another of Thoth's functions was to be the messenger of Egypt's gods, the Greeks came to identify him with Hermes, their own divine messenger. After Egypt came under Greek rule in 332BC, Thoth's cult city of Khmun was renamed Hermopolis. And as the Greek god Hermes Trismegistus, Thoth became the centre of a mystery cult all of his own, which still has its followers today.

At the heart of the god's mystique was *The Book of Thoth*, within which the most powerful secrets were locked. But this text was always associated with great danger. There are many tales of people who discovered the book's destructive potential at their own peril. One such victim was Prince Neferkaptah, a character who may have been based on the historical figure of Prince Hardjedef, son of the Old Kingdom pharaoh, Khufu. According to a story written in the Ptolemaic period, Neferkaptah was a powerful magician proficient in the knowledge of magical texts. He was a passionate reader of the papyri archived in temple libraries throughout the kingdom. But he was also humane: he loved deeply his sister-wife Ahwere and was devoted to their young son Merib.

One day, as Neferkaptah studied inscriptions on the wall of a temple, he heard laughter and

A 3000-year-old papyrus records a charm against headaches. By Greek times, such spells were credited to the god Thoth.

Thrice-Great Thoth

The god Thoth fascinated the Greeks, who identified him with their messenger god Hermes, and gave him the epithet Trismegistus, *meaning "thrice-great". The Greeks were particularly captivated by the elusive* Book of Thoth, *described by Clement of Alexandria as forty-two secret books of wisdom. These texts, housed in temple archives, were regarded as the work of Thoth himself.*

These books were in fact rewritten as the *Hermetica* by Graeco-Roman visitors during the Ptolemaic and Roman periods, from the first to the third centuries AD, and so contained a mix of Egyptian myth and Greek philosophy, with the addition of alchemical and astrological lore and powerful spells.

Many believed the texts to be immeasurably ancient, and steeped in Egyptian wisdom that had been passed down through the millennia from one initiate to another. To their adherents, the writings of Hermes Trismegistus (Thoth) amounted to nothing less than the universal secret of life.

The *Hermetica* included elaborate spells for imprisoning demons, and magical charms to make statues speak or prophesy, as well as texts on classical subjects such as astronomy, medicine, geography, and even rudimentary chemistry. These were treated in a philosophical language that was mostly taken from contemporary Greek thinking but was widely believed to be far older.

Throughout the Middle Ages, the books appealed enormously to scholars and alchemists from all traditions – Muslims and Jews as well as Christians. For example, the Polish astronomer Copernicus, who established that the earth orbited the sun, claimed that he had reached his conclusions partly as a result of his study of Hermetic writings.

turned to see a wizened old priest cackling at him. When Neferkaptah asked him what he found so amusing, the priest replied: "Why do you waste time on these worthless spells? I know where you can find the great *Book of Thoth* itself. Its first spell will give

you power over the sky above and the earth below, and control over the birds and the beasts and the fishes of the sea. The second spell will give you power over the Land of the Dead: it will bring the dead back to life and allow you to see the gods themselves." Neferkaptah felt that he simply had to have the book and asked the priest what he would have to do to obtain it. In exchange for one hundred silver pieces and two priests to serve his *ka* after death (see page 96), the old man gave him the following information: "The book is lying on the bed of the Nile near Coptos, in an iron box. Inside the iron box is one of copper; and in the copper box is another of juniper wood. Within that, there is a box of ebony, and then another of ivory, which contains a silver box within which you will find a golden box. The book is in the box of gold. But there are six miles of writhing snakes and countless scorpions guarding these boxes."

Neferkaptah was confident that his magician's skills would overcome the stings of snakes and scorpions. Without hesitation, he rushed home to his wife and son, and took them with him to Coptos by ship. There, he used a multitude of spells to discover the whereabouts of the box on the river bed. He then employed some especially powerful magic to divide the waters of the Nile,

His arms outstretched in supplication, a kneeling priest performs a ritual. Priests were held to have magic powers by virtue of their status. This bronze figurine is from the 21st Dynasty.

and at last saw the box marooned on the dry bed, and surrounded with snakes as the old priest had suggested.

His spells successfully held the venomous creatures at bay, except for an enormous snake that was tightly coiled around the box. With a mighty blow from his bronze axe, Neferkaptah chopped the monster in half. But the creature was supernatural and the two halves promptly rejoined. The snake attacked the magician-prince and began to choke him in its embrace.

Again and again the prince sliced at the serpent; again and again the fragments rejoined. Finally, Neferkaptah thought of throwing a handful of sand scooped from the dry river bed over the monster's cut flesh before the two halves could come together. The creature's healing magic was broken at last, and the writhing serpent died in agony. Neferkaptah opened the iron box, then with frantic haste tore through the remaining boxes until at last he held *The Book of Thoth* in his hands.

He read the first spell immediately, and sure enough, he now held the powers of enchantment over the whole earth, as the old priest had told him. Suddenly, he was able to understand the language of the birds, the beasts and even the fishes. Exultant, he went on to read the second spell. The sun, the moon and the stars were revealed to him in their true forms, as was the Land of the Dead, and he could perceive the gods themselves.

Still trembling with excitement, he returned to his ship and ordered the crew to row back to Coptos. While his wife was reading the two great

119

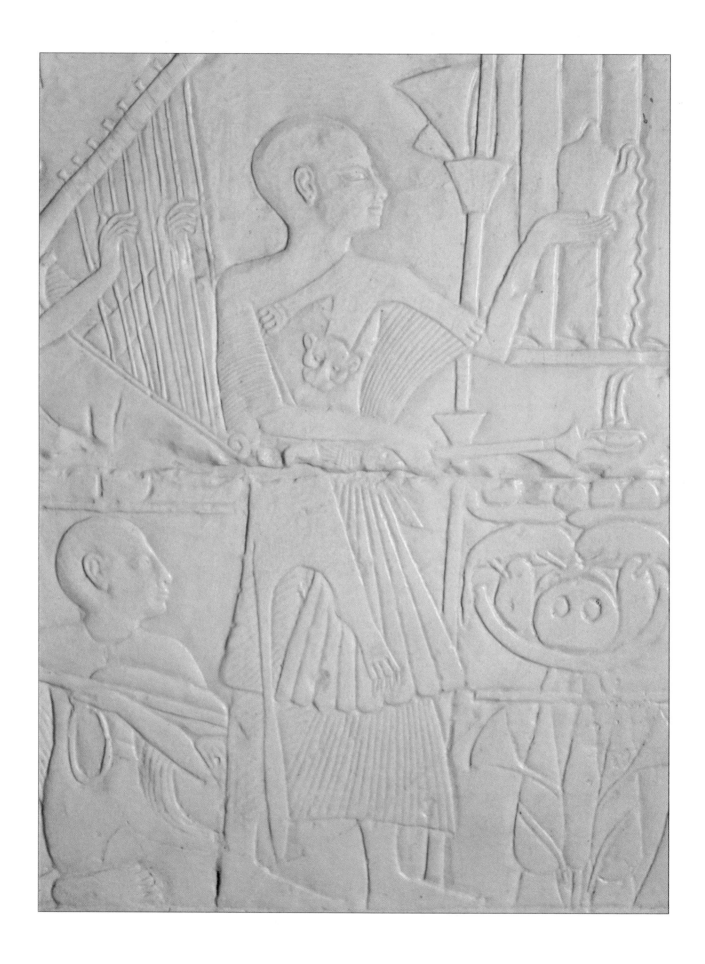

spells, Neferkaptah copied the words on to fresh papyrus, soaked it in beer and crumbled it into a bowl of water, which he swallowed at a gulp. He became drunk with power, and in that condition set sail for his home in Memphis.

But the gods were extremely displeased by Neferkaptah's behaviour. Thoth himself complained to Re and demanded a suitable punishment for the man who had slain the monster guardian of his book and taken the book's power for himself. Re agreed with Thoth, and a terrible punishment was chosen.

To start with, young Merib, Neferkaptah's son, was killed. Cursed by Re, he fell into the waters of the Nile and drowned. At once, his father recited Thoth's second spell. But Merib did not come back to life: instead, his body floated to the surface and his mouth opened for a final time to pronounce the wrath of Re on his father. Then he fell silent forever. Distraught, his parents rowed back to Coptos so that Merib could be embalmed while a suitable tomb was prepared to receive his mummified body.

No sooner had they returned to Memphis than Ahwere, Neferkaptah's wife, became the next victim of the curse. Like her son, she was struck down and splashed into the river. When Neferkaptah tried to use the second spell, Ahwere's corpse could do no more than repeat Re's judgement as her own dead child had done. Crazed with grief, Neferkaptah went back to Coptos and buried his wife beside his son in the newly completed tomb.

As the despairing prince set off alone on the boat journey to Memphis, he was stricken with remorse. "How can I return alone, alive, to my father the king, and tell him what has happened?" he moaned. Unable to control his grief, he tied *The Book of Thoth* tightly to his body, and hurled himself into the river. His corpse was not found until his ship arrived in Memphis, when the bereft king saw the remains of his son tangled in its rudders.

The king ordered the fateful book to be buried forever with his son. But, despite the terrible example of Neferkaptah, others would come in a later time to seek out the text – only to pay a similar price for their daring (see page 111).

The Elements of Magic

While no man or woman could match the power of the gods, everyday magic was still very much the business of mortals – especially those who had

Right: A quartzite statuette of the lector priest Petamenope contemplates one of the thousands of sacred scrolls entrusted to him during his lifetime. Petamenope lived around 700BC.

Opposite: A lector priest makes an offering to the gods. Such men were considered masters of all the lore that Egypt possessed – above all else, they were adept in magic.

mastered the power of the written word, although these were few in number.

Before the advent of writing in Egypt, magical traditions must have been passed down by word of mouth. But very early in the land's long history, spells and rituals that had been preserved in the oral tradition were recorded in writing – an art generally reckoned to be profoundly magical in itself. The sacred texts had to be guarded by those who understood them, and men who rose to the office of *hery-heb*, "lector priest", inevitably came to hold a very high status in a country where it is believed that less than one per cent of the population were able to read.

Lector priests were respected for their learning but even more so for their knowledge of magic. They were responsible for communicating sacred texts during religious and funerary ceremonies. They also had a reputation for accurately interpreting dreams, as they had access to the "Dream Books" – papyri which described dreams and explained their meanings, indicating whether they boded well or ill.

Some lector priests served the king directly, either as trusted palace advisors or else as diplomatic envoys. More often, however, these priests seem to have been employed in the "House of Life" (*per-ankh*), an educational institution attached to most temples, in which libraries were established to store great numbers of religious texts. Here priests studied the secrets of the scrolls and absorbed arcane magical lore. Sometimes they sold their services outside the House of Life, performing important rituals for those members of the laity who were able to afford them.

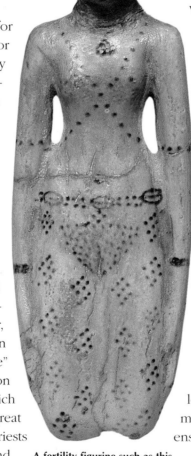

A fertility figurine such as this Middle Kingdom example made in faience (glazed earthenware) would have been used by women as a good luck charm during childbirth. This tattooed figure is nude except for the elaborate hip girdle.

Of great importance to ordinary Egyptians was the *sunu*, usually translated as "physician" – although the ancient Egyptians made little distinction between medicine as a science and medicine as a magical practice. The earliest surviving medical papyri date from around 1825BC, although they refer to methods already known for centuries. All Egyptian doctors, whether priests or not, were trained in the medical technology of the age, which was advanced for the time.

The priests of Sekhmet had a particular responsibility to deal with disease, which was thought to be propagated by the goddess Isis herself, whom they sought to control through regular worship.

Medicine was practised not on its own but in conjunction with incantations and ritual to further its effect. Some of the ingredients for these spells – such as the herbs henbane and mandrake – would have had straightforward pharmacological effects, while more bizarre ingredients – dirt from a patient's fingernails, or mouse faeces – were used in the belief that small quantities of negative substances can produce positive effects in a patient's body. Urine and dung were often included in the potions because they were believed to repel the demons who created illness and suffering.

Patients themselves were often less concerned with the contents of magical potions than they were with ensuring that the appropriate invocations were made to the appropriate god, and that the correct procedure was followed for the particular condition to be cured. This was particularly so when an ailment did not have a visible cause. Thus bone-setting, for example, was largely a matter of following medical procedures; whereas treating unexplained headaches required reference to the texts for relevant spells.

There was a rationale behind the ingredients that were included in medicinal spells, as well as the routines that they followed. The powerful smell of garlic, for example, was used to keep snakes and scorpions at bay. Honey was used to relieve burns and wounds, as it is to this day by some practitioners of alternative medicine. And a purely symbolic methodology suggested that a spell designed as an antidote to poison should be said over a knotted rope so that the poison would be "tied up".

Weshptah's Misfortune

There are a number of mythic tales of doctors and lector priests as necromancers, performing miraculous acts by exploiting the powers of the gods to raise corpses from the dead. However, their powers were far from infallible. The unfortunate Weshptah, for example, who was vizier and chief architect to King Neferirkare around 2440BC, could not be saved from death, according to a tale recorded in Weshptah's fragmentary tomb inscription. This relates how the king was inspecting his latest building project, accompanied by his retinue of courtiers. Despite the king's compliments about the work, Weshptah paid him no heed. The king turned to reproach Weshptah, who instantly fell to the ground – not in apologetic abasement but because he had suffered some kind of stroke and was incapacitated.

Weshptah was taken back to the palace, and the lector priests and doctors arrived with the intention of curing him. But a miracle was not forthcoming: the best that the king could do for his architect was to organize his burial and have a special ebony coffin constructed on his behalf as a mark of respect.

Another valued magician was the scorpion-charmer, a man who claimed the title *kherep Serqet*, meaning "one who has power over the scorpion goddess Serqet", and who dealt with poisonous creatures. This position was usually part-time and held by a doctor, a lector priest or even a labourer – one such whose name was recorded was a certain Amenmose of the Theban village of Deir el-Medina. These people were always in demand, because poisonous snakes and scorpions were a constant menace to all Egyptians. Men who worked amid the sun-scorched stones of temple or tomb construction sites were particularly at risk, and there was often a scorpion-charmer assigned to a particular workforce, or to a military expedition into the desert.

The scorpion goddess Serqet stands guard over the coffin of Tutankhamun (1333–1323BC). Serqet was called upon in spells that cured stings and bites. She was also known as a protectress of the Canopic jars in which a mummy's entrails were stored.

123

A Magical Universe

Heka was believed to dwell in objects as well as individuals. Amuletic jewellery, for example, was inscribed with magical texts and symbols which usually included protective spells to ward off evil spirits (see pages 20–21). Other objects, such as the magic "wands" used during ritual, were believed to reinforce the effect of religious ceremonials.

At their simplest, amulets were made from nothing more than an inscribed pebble; but for the rich, Egypt's craftsmen were more than capable of creating exquisite, much-treasured scarabs of every valuable material. An amulet's power could come from its design, colour or rarity as well as from inscribed words, and any combination of these elements gave it *heka*.

One of the most important of the various forms of amulet was the *wedjat* ("divine eye") of the sky god Horus whose left eye was lunar and whose right eye was solar. The lunar eye, damaged by his uncle Seth according to myth, was restored by the goddess Hathor and therefore came to represent wholeness and healing. But it was the god Thoth who brought back from Nubia the eye of Horus that was associated with the sun. Therefore, the *wedjat* eventually came to symbolize and contain the healing powers of both the lunar and the solar eye (see pages 28 and 57).

Magic "wands" used in rituals date from about 2800BC. Usually carved from hippopotamus ivory, they appear to have been modelled on the throwing sticks which farmers used to chase off birds. Wild birds were a common symbol for chaos, and the control of wild creatures represented a powerful victory of the forces of order over the forces of evil. The latter were particularly potent during childbirth, so the wand was often placed over the unborn child during pregnancy rituals. The wand seems to have represented the powers of the hippopotamus goddess, Tawaret, who watched over mothers and is usually shown on its surface with other helpful deities. Tawaret usually appears with the body of a hippopotamus, a crocodile's tail and a woman's sagging breasts. Her symbolic presence was believed to ensure a safe delivery.

Early examples have animal heads carved at each end, but otherwise these wands were plain in design. Through the third millennium BC, however,

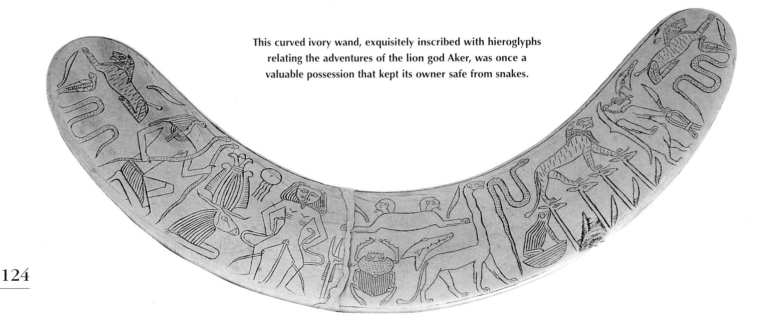

This curved ivory wand, exquisitely inscribed with hieroglyphs relating the adventures of the lion god Aker, was once a valuable possession that kept its owner safe from snakes.

Siosire and the Sorcerer of Nubia

One day, before the court of King Rameses II in Memphis, a haughty Nubian appeared and issued a challenge to the best scholar of Egypt, testing his abilities in magic.

Holding a sealed papyrus up to the king, he asked "Can anyone here read this letter without opening it? If there is none wise enough to do so, all of Nubia shall know of Egypt's shame."

Perplexed, Rameses called for Prince Setna, the most learned of his sons. Setna, too, was baffled; but, rather than admit defeat, he asked for ten days' grace to wrestle with the problem.

Setna had no idea how to read the strange letter, and simply fretted anxiously at home, lying on his bed and hiding his face in his garments. His wife asked what was wrong, but he gruffly told her that it was nothing a woman could help with. When his young son Siosire tried to comfort him, he said "You are only twelve. A child cannot help me here."

Eventually, however, Siosire persuaded his father to explain the problem. "But that's easy," laughed the boy. "I can do that!" To prove it, he asked Setna to bring a papyrus scroll from his bookchest. As the boy promised, he was able to read it while his father held it still rolled up.

The next day Siosire went with his father to meet the pharaoh and the arrogant Nubian. At once, the boy proceeded to read from the scroll tied to the Nubian's belt. And what he read shocked the court.

It was a tale from the distant past, one and a half thousand years before, when the Prince of Nubia had used the powers of his great magician Sa-Neheset to bring Egypt's pharaoh to the Nubian court. There he received a brutal and shameful beating. The pharaoh in turn sought magical aid from his own master-magician, Sa-Paneshe, and the struggle between the two nations turned into a battle of wills between two great magicians. In the end, Sa-Paneshe triumphed and the humiliated Nubian sorcerer swore by all his nation's gods not to return to Egypt for one and a half thousand years.

The young Siosire reached the end of his reading. "Now, O king," said the boy, "I can tell you why this Nubian is here. For he is Sa-Neheset, born again after one and a half thousand years. But I, too, have been reborn: I am Sa-Paneshe, and I challenge him once again!" For hours the two sorcerers fought spell against spell, the one seeking to destroy Egypt's court, the other to save it. At last, Siosire (or Sa-Paneshe) sent a fire-spell the other could not resist, and Sa-Neheset was consumed in flames.

Victorious Sa-Paneshe vanished too, called back to the underworld by Osiris.

In the cataclysmic last act of a 1500-year-long drama, the Nubian sorcerer Sa-Neheset and his scroll of spells are engulfed in the flames summoned by his rival, the Egyptian master-magician Sa-Paneshe.

they became more elaborate in appearance. From about 2100BC, wands began to appear engraved with pictures and magical spells. The same inscribed text tended to recur: "Words spoken by these gods: we have come to give protection ... "

The same symbols that decorate the wands often appeared on domestic articles such as head-rests (used as pillows), so that their protective power would continue throughout the night. Besides Tawaret, one of the most common deities depicted on such items was the dwarf-god Bes. Both Bes and Tawaret were mainly house-hold gods, who were believed to be able to frighten away demons.

Protection might also be required against the dead when they appeared as the sinister *mut* spirits (see pages 109–10). Eventually, even the *akhu* (blessed souls) came to be regarded as potential sources of unrest, and so families would make regular offerings to their ancestors who would be powerful allies in the spirit world if sufficiently placated.

Curses had a long history in Egypt. Often practised by inscribing the names of enemies of the state on clay pots, or making figurines of them, which could be ceremonially smashed, cursing was part of the state religions as practised in the temples. The real enemy, it was hoped, would share the fate of the image. A wax doll in the shape of an enemy, augmented with locks of his hair, or trimmings from his nails, might be tortured or even melted, for the same reason.

Such techniques were open to abuse. In one celebrated case during the reign of Rameses III (1194–1163BC), a conspirator consulted one of the books of magic from the royal library to make wax dolls that he hoped to manipulate in order to cripple the royal guard. However, the king himself used more conventional forms of counter-intelligence to detect the plot orchestrated against him, and the perpetrators were executed or forced to kill themselves.

Perhaps the best-documented period of Egyptian magical practices stretches from the Greek invasion until the Roman conquest (332–30BC). The Greeks had long been fascinated by Egypt, and under the Ptolemaic Dynasty there was an upsurge of interest in its magical practices.

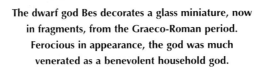

The dwarf god Bes decorates a glass miniature, now in fragments, from the Graeco-Roman period. Ferocious in appearance, the god was much venerated as a benevolent household god.

However, the Romans were less impressed by magic than were their Greek predecessors. They prohibited many of the services offered by Egyptian magicians, such as death curses or spells to destroy a marriage; and it was probably because he thought they had seditious overtones that the Emperor Augustus had many thousands of magical texts set alight.

However, in trying to suppress Egyptian magic Rome's imperial police made little headway. They merely encouraged an already secretive profession to become even more elusive, and as magic, once a routine aspect of life in Egypt, went further underground, so its reputation grew. Spells were still being written and distributed as late as the third century AD, and with the cult of Hermes Trismegistus (see page 118), versions of Egyptian magic passed into the Jewish Cabbala, the arcane beliefs of medieval Europe, and beyond. There is no doubt (although its form may have changed almost beyond recognition) that vestiges of Egypt's magic remain with us in esoteric circles to this day.

The Enchanted Island

Returning from an unsuccessful trade mission in Nubia, an Egyptian envoy bemoaned his disappointment – provoking a sailor to recount a tale that began with tragedy but ended happily.

A 19th-century painting by David Roberts depicting the temple complex at Philae – an island in the Nile that the Egyptians regarded with special reverence.

An unnamed sailor was on a voyage on the Red Sea, destined for the royal mines. His sixty-metre-long vessel was well-appointed, and stoutly manned by one hundred and twenty crewmen. But a sudden squall overwhelmed the ship, and she vanished beneath the waves, as did everyone on board – except the narrator.

The survivor found himself washed ashore on an island that had all the appearance of an earthly paradise: it was overflowing with fruits and vegetables, and all the fish and fowl the hungry sailor could wish for. However, a giant serpent, with a body of gold and eyebrows of lapis lazuli, also lived there. The monster threatened the sailor with instant incineration if he did not explain his arrival. But the sailor was rigid with fear. The serpent took him to its lair, whereupon the sailor recounted his tale. The serpent then told its own sorry story. "Once, there were seventy-five snakes here," it said, "including all my kin. But a burning star fell and killed all of them except me. Fate will be kinder to you. A ship will arrive in four months, and you will return safely to your home."

The ship arrived as the snake had promised, and the sailor boarded it, laden with gifts from the now friendly monster. On his return home, the king was so pleased that he made the voyager a royal attendant and granted him many servants.

Royal Tales of Enchantment

Egypt's kings were credited with magical power, and in the *Pyramid Texts* the king is called a "possessor of magic". Royal personages often feature in stories about magic, and a wise king always treated his magicians with respect.

A text from the Old Kingdom has survived which shows how magic could be used for relatively light-hearted purposes, as well as for serious matters. The Westcar Papyrus, as it is known after the Englishman who eventually acquired it, contains three complete tales. These are related by King Khufu's three sons to their father and his courtiers. Khufu (also known as Cheops), his son Khephren, and his grandson Menkaure, were the builders of the Giza Pyramids (see pages 92–93). Although other tales are told in this papyrus, these are all incomplete, and their outcome remains a mystery to us today. Taken together, the stories in the papyrus not only provide fascinating details about kingship and magic, but indicate the strength of the oral tradition in ancient Egypt. Although originally intended for the pleasure of the king and his courtiers, these stories can now enlighten modern readers in many nuances of daily life in the pharaonic court.

The first of the complete stories is set in the days of Khufu's ancestor King Nebka, when certain curious events took place during a royal visit one day to the temple of Ptah. King Nebka had stopped off *en route* to visit his chief lector priest, Webaoner. Among the king's retinue was a handsome young man who caught the eye of Webaoner's wife. The woman was immediately infatuated with him, and she later sent him a present of fine clothing as a token of her passion. He was equally smitten with her, and soon the two were arranging illicit meetings in Webaoner's summerhouse, where they drank wine together and indulged in amorous play.

But it is impossible to guard a secret in a house filled with servants. The chief steward discovered their clandestine liaison, and reported it to his master. Naturally, Webaoner was enraged, and as one of Egypt's most renowned magicians resolved to use his magic to avenge himself.

A representation of the crocodile god Sobek gleams in bronze and electrum. Sobek was respected enough for several pharaohs to name themselves after him.

Imhotep: From Man to God

In his lifetime, Imhotep was Grand Vizier to King Djoser, chief scribe of the court, and architect of the king's enormous pyramid at Saqqara, which was the first monumental stone construction in the world. Without the blessing of royal blood, no one could hope to rise higher.

After his death, however, Imhotep became even greater. With the passage of time, the details of his master's life faded: apart from what has been found in Djoser's pyramid, we know almost nothing, by contrast, of the mighty king. But Imhotep was long remembered by his fellow-scribes as the master of their craft, and the composer of many great literary works. As one papyrus suggests, "A book is of more value than the house of a master-builder or a tomb in the western desert." By the Middle and New Kingdoms, Imhotep was credited with having written a work entitled *A Book of Instruction*, although no such work is known to have survived.

By the Late Period (712–332 BC), small bronze statues were being made that showed him seated, with a scroll in his lap, wearing a linen kilt.

By the Ptolemaic period, the vizier had acquired further status by becoming "son of Ptah", the creator god of Memphis. He advanced to the rank of a god, with a cult of his own centred around temples at Saqqara and Thebes where he was worshipped as the epitome of wisdom. Scribes and craftsmen alike sought the god's help in their work. He also had a reputation as a great healer, and so was merged in Ptolemaic times with the Greek god of medicine, Asclepius.

A votive statue of Imhotep, patron of scribes and scholars, represents him holding the open scroll that served as his trademark.

Webaoner ordered servants to bring him his special chest made of ebony and electrum (an alloy combining gold and silver), in which he kept some of the tools of his trade. He took some wax, moulded it into the shape of a crocodile "seven hands' breadths long", and recited incantations until the model was ready to be used. Webaoner waited until evening, when the young man went to bathe in the lector priest's own lake, then ordered a steward to throw the wax crocodile into the water beside him.

Instantly, the inanimate wax model turned into a ferocious living beast, seven cubits (three and a half metres) long. Seizing the man between its jaws, the crocodile disappeared beneath the surface of the water. The magician was so pleased by his success that he asked King Nebka to come and witness the young man's predicament. With the king looking on, he summoned the crocodile to surface with the struggling youth still crushed in its awful mouth. He then released the young man by returning the monster to an inert state as a small wax figure. The king was both impressed and delighted by Webaoner's magic.

The luckless victim's reprieve, however, was short-lived. When Webaoner described the unlawful affair between the young man and his wife, King Nebka became furious too. At the pharaoh's command, Webaoner reanimated the wax crocodile. The enormous reptile snatched the adulterer and disappeared beneath the lake forever. Webaoner's faithless wife also met a terrible fate. At the king's command, she was burnt to death, and her ashes were thrown into the water where she joined her lover. The message of this story was that magicians, able to bring death upon wrongdoers, were to be respected and feared.

The papyrus goes on to say that Khufu was so pleased by the story of King Nebka that he ordered lavish offerings to be made at the king's tomb, with further rewards for the shade of the mighty lector priest Webaoner.

Prince Hardjedef's Tale

After a second tale told by the middle son, Baufre, about King Snofru and a beautiful pendant (see opposite), Prince Hardjedef, the third son, entertained his father with a story that had a less satisfactory outcome for the monarch. Prince Hardjedef was reputedly the wisest among the three princes. He announced to the court that he would recount a tale not from the distant past but one involving people actually present.

Hardjedef's subject was a mighty magician called Djedi who was one hundred and ten years old, and considered to be the wonder of Egypt. Djedi could unite a severed head with its body, and make a lion follow meekly behind him. He also knew the number of the secret chambers in the temple of Thoth. This, according to Hardjedef, immediately aroused Khufu's interest. He had long hoped to model his own tomb on those secret chambers, so straightaway he ordered the magician to be brought before him.

In response to his father's command, Prince Hardjedef set off with three boats along the Nile to find Djedi's village. He soon returned, with the old man beside him in the first boat, his children following in the second boat, and plenty of magical books stowed in the third. Djedi made the customary obeisances and Khufu received him with curiosity. But when the king asked the magician why he had never before placed his magical power at the service of the royal family, Djedi gave a humble reply: "He who is summoned comes. O king, my Lord, I was summoned and I have come."

Next, the king asked Djedi whether it was really true that he could join a severed head to its body and return life to the corpse. When the magician replied that he did indeed have that power, Khufu ordered a criminal to be brought from the royal prison so that the king could witness the miracle performed before his eyes. To the king's annoyance, however, Djedi refused to perform his magic on a human being; so instead a goose was brought from the royal kitchens and decapitated. Sure enough, Djedi cast a spell and the bird's body walked across the hall to its head, which promptly leapt back onto its neck. This trick was then applied to a duck, followed by an ox. Finally, Djedi displayed further powers before the king's court by taming a ravenous lion.

Khufu then demanded to know the number of the secret chambers of Thoth's temple. But the answer was not forthcoming. "I do not know the number, O King," replied Djedi, "but I do know where it may be found. The secret lies in a chest of flint in the Temple of Heliopolis." "Then bring it to me at once," said the king. But Khufu's request was not that simple. "It is not I who shall bring it to you," said the magician; "it must be brought by the eldest of three children who are now in the womb of the woman Redjedet, fathered by the god Re himself." Djedi went on to prophesy: "These children, the god has said, will be kings in this land." Khufu was aghast at this suggestion that his own line might not rule, but Djedi reassured him: "First your son, then his son, then one of them will reign." The prophecy was fulfilled: the children of Redjedet did go on to become the first kings of Egypt's Fifth Dynasty.

Khufu never did learn the number of the secret chambers in Thoth's temple. Djedi, however, was installed in apartments in Prince Hardjedef's house, and assigned a daily allowance of "a thousand loaves of bread, a hundred jugs of beer, one ox and a hundred bundles of vegetables".

The Turquoise Pendant

In the second of the three tales of wonder contained in the Westcar Papyrus, Prince Baufre tells of his father's father, King Snofru, and Snofru's lector priest Djadjaemankh.

The day was especially hot. Bored to distraction, Snofru summoned Djadjaemankh, one of his lector priests, and demanded entertainment. Djadjaemankh ("He who carries the ritual book") devised a plan. The king should go out in a boat on the palace lake, where he could cool off and enjoy the beauty of the scenery. To add to his enjoyment, it was suggested that the boat be rowed by twenty of the most attractive girls from the royal harem.

The king's downcast visage brightened at once. "Let the boat be fitted with gilded oars of ebony and sandalwood," he ordered enthusiastically. The girls were told to replace their regular linen shifts with nets of faience beads that scarcely concealed their curves.

At first, all went well. The king reclined happily, enjoying the flowers, the birds and the fish of his lake, but devoting most of his attention to the efforts of his scantily-clad crew. After a while, however, the leading rower inadvertently dropped the fine turquoise pendant she wore in her braided hair into the lake. She cried out in dismay, and the rowing stopped. The poor girl was distraught at her loss. Indulgently, the king offered to replace the lost pendant from his own store of turquoise, but the girl insisted that nothing other than the return of her own ornament would satisfy her.

"Djadjaemankh!" called the king. "Solve the problem." The lector priest bowed, and at once uttered a powerful spell. Instantly, the waters of the lake rolled back to reveal the amulet lying safely

Found in Tutankhamun's tomb, an exquisitely-crafted pendant of the 14th century BC. Such a pectoral would not only have served as a beautiful ornament: it would have been worn as a charm against evil.

on the dry bed. Djadjaemankh retrieved it, climbed back to the lake bank and used another spell to return the lake to its former level.

Snofru was deeply impressed by Djadjaemankh's powers and rewarded the servant with riches. The girl put her amulet back in her hair, and the rowing party continued throughout a long and happy afternoon.

Egyptian mummies were also shipped abroad, where they were treated with disrespect by people such as Thomas Pettigrew, an English antiquary and surgeon, who performed post-mortems on Egyptian corpses in front of paying audiences. "It was a task of no little difficulty," he reported of one of his shows in 1833, "and required considerable force to separate the bandages from the body; levers were absolutely necessary." It is fortunate that when he applied to "autopsy" the British Museum's collection of mummies his request was turned down.

After the clumsy incursions of early Egyptologists, a new generation of archaeologists played a role in conservation. W. M. Flinders Petrie, who began work in Egypt in 1881, heralded the birth of revolutionary archaeological methods. "Conservation must be [the archaeologist's] first duty," he wrote. "To uncover a monument, and leave it to perish by exposure or by plundering, to destroy thus what had lasted for thousands of years, and might last for thousands to come, is a crime." Living in a tent, with "a pinch of books", and "London food sent out to him from Civil Service stores," Petrie ensured that each site was excavated with care. By the time of his death in 1942, he and his followers had slowed the flood of unbridled discovery to a trickle of careful analysis.

Art Nouveau style looked to nature and exotic cultures for inspiration in the design of architecture, interiors and furniture. This detail from a cabinet made in Budapest in about 1907 shows a goddess whose wings and headdress are derived from Egyptian representations of Isis.

The Early Archaeologists

Following Napoleon's invasion of Egypt, scientists and scholars descended on the land in an attempt to tabulate, uncover and – far too frequently – remove its antiquities. This resulted in an uneasy combination of archaeological inquiry and blatant treasure-hunting.

The colossal statues of Rameses II outside a temple at Abu Simbel caught the imagination of artists like David Roberts, who was enchanted by Egypt as Western archeologists uncovered its treasures in the nineteenth century.

Among the first official archaeologists were Bernardino Drovetti and Henry Salt, the French and British consuls in Egypt during the 1820s. Often at loggerheads, they reached a gentleman's agreement whereby everything on the Nile's west bank was the province of Britain, and everything on the east bank the domain of France – although in the case of particularly prized sites it was a matter of first-past-the-post. They amassed valuable collections of artefacts but their analytical methods were far from precise.

One of Salt's agents, an Italian by the name of Giovanni Battista Belzoni, recalled entering a tomb full of mummies on the west bank at Thebes. Having struggled through overpowering clouds of dust and the stench of "mummy effluvia", he decided to sit and recover. "But when my weight bore on the body of an Egyptian," he wrote, "it crushed like a band-box. I naturally had recourse to my hands to sustain my weight, but they found no better support, so that I sank altogether among the broken mummies with a crash of bones, rags and wooden cases, which raised such a dust as kept me motionless for a quarter of an hour, waiting till it subsided again."

Belzoni, for all his carelessness, was not without dedication. He actually lived in one tomb during the period it took him to make wax casts of its inscriptions. Nevertheless, he ranked among a growing number of adventurers whose main aim was to seize ancient objects for themselves or their employers, with no regard to archaeological context. Even the more reputable Egyptologists took an haphazard approach, often attracting the label "gunpowder archaeologists" because they used explosives to open many tombs.

In 1835 the Egyptian government halted the more spectacular desecrations by insisting that every potential treasure-hunter apply for permission to dig, and by banning the unlicensed export of Egyptian antiquities. Although fallible, these measures stalled the wholesale removal of ancient Egyptian artefacts from their country of origin.

In this new atmosphere monitored by officials the work of dedicated Egyptologists came to the fore. Men such as Sir John Gardener Wilkinson, who spent twelve years and his own funds recording archaeological sites and translating texts, ensured that Egypt's treasures were dutifully restored and respected.

Egyptian style was a major influence on Art Deco, a design movement that flourished in the late 1920s and the 1930s. The architect of this building in Miami, USA, based its shape on temple pylons and its decoration on tomb paintings.

However, spectacular treasures were still available, as the opening of Tutankhamun's tomb in 1922 displayed. A new methodology was implemented, and it took ten years to excavate the boy-king's burial chamber and its contents (see pages 112–13). In the decades to come, the world community, acting in concert with the Egyptian government, poured millions of dollars into rescuing the remains of ancient Egypt.

Nevertheless, the more Egypt became part of an increasingly industrial world, the more its heritage suffered. Tourists arrived in thousands to trample up and down the pyramids, often inscribing their names on the blocks. After the opening in 1869 of the Suez Canal, linking the Mediterranean and the Red Sea, their numbers swelled dramatically. Foreigners, however, were not the only ones to blame. In 1902, following the construction of the Aswan dam at the Nile cataracts, many monuments in Nubia were submerged for most of the year. And in the late 1950s, when the Egyptian government approved the construction of a new Aswan dam which would create a lake four hundred and eighty-two kilometres long, it looked as if they would be lost altogether. Only by an unprecedented international effort were most of the major temples dismantled and rebuilt on higher ground before the dam's completion in 1965. Even so, many archaeological sites disappeared beneath the waters.

Egypt's Impact on Western Art

Following Napoleon's invasion, Egyptian motifs were added enthusiastically to Europe's artistic repertoire. A new "Empire style", which combined elements of Roman, Greek and Egyptian design, swept the continent. Winged lions formed the arms of chairs; sphinx heads were placed atop columns to decorate the fronts of bureaux, bookcases and cabinets; pyramids became an accepted item among other mantelpiece features. This Egyptomania found its most costly manifestation in a sixty-six-piece dinner service of Sèvres porcelain, commissioned by Napoleon. Each plate depicted different views of the wonders to be found in that ancient land. Throughout the nineteenth century Egypt was celebrated in diverse forms: Shelley's poem "Ozymandias" and Verdi's opera *Aida*, commissioned by Ismail Pasha to commemorate the opening of the Cairo opera house in 1871, were both inspired by Egypt. In the 1930s Egyptian motifs appeared once again in the Art Deco movement. The clean lines of the pyramids appealed to '30s designers, who also incorporated more exotic insignia such as the Eye of Re and the lotus in many pieces of jewellery.

In the late 1980s the French Ministry of Culture paid homage to Egyptian architecture by constructing a steel and glass pyramid in the courtyard of the Louvre Museum. The pyramid and the Eye of Re have also been given worldwide currency on the back of the US dollar bill.

All the discoveries and clarifications of modern scholarship have done nothing to diminish the mystique of Egypt. Extravagant theories claim that the sphinx and the pyramids are far older than has ever been thought. According to some, the sphinx displays erosion patterns that could only have been caused by prolonged rainfall – an occurrence which last happened in about 13,000BC. The pyramids, others say, were built to reflect an astronomical cycle which can only be measured in thousands of years. Moreover, their construction is said to have been beyond the ancient Egyptians – and to be almost impossible even by modern standards. A few extreme theorists have looked for the pyramid-builders in the story of the lost and legendary Atlantis. A more apocalyptic view is that the pyramids map a particular stellar configuration that regularly coincides with global catastrophes, and that they contain the secret of the apocalypse.

However bizarre some of these theories may be, their very existence serves to remind us that ancient Egypt, far from being dead, continues to exert an uncanny pull on our imaginations.

During the 1980s the Louvre Museum in Paris underwent a radical reconstruction. This glass and steel pyramid (which is illuminated at night) was designed by I. M. Pei to dominate Napoleon's court in the centre of the gallery, providing a monumental entrance for visitors.

Glossary of Gods and Key Terms

akh the blessed dead – the ultimate form that the deceased took in the afterlife once its **ka** and **ba** were united. In later times the term also described a malevolent spirit.

Ammut the hybrid monster who ate the sinful hearts of those who failed the judgement of **Osiris**.

Amun the supreme creator god of Thebes who combined with the sun god **Re** to become Amun-Re, King of the Gods, by New Kingdom times (1550–1070BC).

ankh "life". Represented as a looped cross hieroglyph.

Anubis the jackal god of mummification and the guardian of cemeteries.

Apis the sacred bull of Memphis, regarded as the manifestation of **Ptah** when living and **Osiris** once dead.

Apophis the serpent god of the underworld representing the forces of chaos.

Astarte a warrior goddess of Near Eastern origin. One of the wives of **Seth**.

Aten the sun disc worshipped as a deity in the 18th Dynasty (1550–1307BC), most notably by Amenhotep IV who replaced the cult of Amun-Re with that of the **Aten**, and changed his own name to Akhenaten.

Atum an ancient creator god worshipped at Heliopolis and gradually merged with the sun god **Re** to form Atum-Re.

ba the personality of an individual, generally portrayed as a human-headed bird. The **ba** undertook the perilous journey through the afterlife before finally uniting with the **ka** spirit to become an **akh**.

Bastet a cat goddess worshipped at the Delta town of Bubastis (Tell Basta).

benben the sacred stone of Heliopolis which represented the mound of creation.

Benu a sacred bird associated with the **benben** stone, and the Greek phoenix.

Bes the dwarf god of the household and protector of women in childbirth.

Buchis a sacred bull of Armant, regarded as the manifestation of **Re** and **Osiris**, who represented the god **Montu**.

Canopic jars the four containers, representing the four sons of **Horus**, which were used to store the internal organs of an eviscerated mummy.

Deshret "red land". The hostile desert.

djed the symbol representing **Osiris**'s backbone and the concept of stability.

Duat the underworld ruled by **Osiris**.

Ennead a group of nine creation deities worshipped at Heliopolis, consisting of **Atum**, his children **Shu** and **Tefnut**, their children **Geb** and **Nut** and their children **Osiris**, **Isis**, **Seth** and **Nephthys**.

Geb the earth god, generally portrayed beneath the arching body of his sister and wife **Nut**.

Hapy an androgynous god of the Nile.

Hathor the goddess of love, beauty and music, represented in both human and bovine form.

Heh the god of infinity, shown kneeling and holding the hieroglyph for "year". One of the **Ogdoad** of Hermopolis.

heka "magic". Those adept in magical practices were referred to as *hekau*.

Heket a goddess of childbirth, represented as a frog.

hery-heb lector priests responsible for temple writings and their recitation during religious ritual.

Horus originally a falcon god of the sky who was the son of **Isis** and **Osiris**. He symbolized kingship following victory over his murderous uncle **Seth**.

ib the Egyptian term for the heart, which was believed to be the seat of wisdom.

Isis the great goddess of magic, whose vital role as wife of **Osiris** and mother of **Horus** established her as the archetypal maternal figure.

ka a term often translated as "soul". It represented an individual's life force.

Kemet the ancient name for Egypt meaning literally "the black land" because it was fertilized by silt from the Nile.

Khepri a creator god who represented the sun god **Re** as he rose each morning. He was symbolized by the scarab beetle.

Khnum the ram-headed creator god who controlled the Nile flood and made each human form and his or her **ka** on his potter's wheel.

Khonsu the young moon god worshipped at Karnak, where his statue was believed to have healing powers.

Ma'at the goddess of truth and cosmic order, instrumental in the judgement of the deceased by **Osiris**.

Meretseger a snake goddess who guarded the royal tombs in the Valley of the Kings, Thebes.

Meskhenet the goddess of childbirth who represented the bricks on which women squatted to give birth.

Min a god of fertility and male sexual potency. He was associated with **Amun**.

Mnevis the sacred black bull of Heliopolis, believed to be the manifestation of the sun god.

Montu the falcon-headed god of war worshipped in the area around Thebes.

Mut a Theban goddess portrayed as a woman with a vulture headdress, consort of **Amun** and mother of **Khonsu**.

mut the restless spirits of the condemned dead who failed the judgement of **Osiris** in the underworld.

Nefertem the god of the lotus and the child of **Ptah** and **Sekhmet**.

Neith an ancient creator deity and warlike archer goddess worshipped in the Delta.

Nekhbet a vulture goddess of Upper Egypt.

Nephthys a funerary goddess and the youngest child of **Geb** and **Nut**. A protector of the dead alongside her sister **Isis**, and the consort to their brother **Seth**.

Nun a god of the primeval waters from which emerged the primeval mound.

Nut a sky goddess pictured as arching her body over her brother **Geb**, god of the earth.

Ogdoad the four pairs of primeval deities in the creation myth of Hermopolis: **Nun** and Naunet (water), Kek and Kauket (darkness), **Heh** and Hauhet (infinity) and **Amun** and Amaunet (hidden power).

Osiris a god identified with resurrection and regarded as lord of the underworld.

Ouroborus a giant serpent who encircled the universe by biting its own tail.

Ptah the Memphite creator god, who thought the universe into being.

Re the supreme sun god, initially based at Heliopolis. His worship extended following amalgamation with **Amun** to form Amun-Re, and other gods such as **Atum** (Atum-Re) and **Horus** (Re-Horakhty). During his nightly journey through the underworld he and **Osiris** were briefly united to become the "Twin Souls".

Renenutet the cobra goddess associated with the harvest.

sa a hieroglyph symbolizing "protection".

Satis a guardian goddess of Egypt's southern frontier at Elephantine, where she was also linked to the Nile inundation.

Sekhmet a powerful lioness goddess and bringer of plague, against which her priests acted appropriately as doctors.

Selket a scorpion goddess with the power to heal.

Seth the god of chaos who murdered his brother **Osiris** and battled with his nephew **Horus**.

shabti a funerary figurine designed to undertake manual work in the afterlife on behalf of its owner.

Shu the god of air who separated the sky (his daughter **Nut**), from the earth (his son **Geb**). One of the Ennead.

Sobek a crocodile god symbolizing royal power who was worshipped at Kom Ombo and Crocodilopolis.

Sothis a goddess personifying the Dog Star, Sirius, whose appearance marked the start of the annual Nile inundation.

Tatjenen a god symbolizing the fertile land revealed by the receding waters of each Nile inundation.

Taweret the hippopotamus goddess of the household and a protector of women in childbirth.

Tefnut the goddess of moisture and the daughter of **Atum**. She and her brother **Shu** were the parents of **Geb** and **Nut**.

Thoth the lunar god of wisdom and writing represented by an ibis bird or a baboon. His major cult centre was Hermopolis (Khemnu).

uraeus the protective cobra emblem worn on the pharaoh's brow. It was believed to spit fire at his enemies.

Wadjet a cobra goddess of Lower Egypt based at Buto in the Delta.

wedjat the Eye of Horus that was believed to have protective qualities and symbolized "wholeness".

Index

Page references in italics refer to picture captions.

Further Reading

Baines, J and J Malek, *Atlas of Ancient Egypt*. Phaidon, London, 1984.
Clayton, P A, *Chronicles of the Pharaohs*. Thames and Hudson, London, 1994.
Desroches-Noblecourt, C, *Tutankhamun: Life and Death of a Pharaoh*. Penguin Books, Harmondsworth, 1989.
El Mahdy, C, *Mummies, Myth and Magic*. Thames and Hudson, London, 1989.
Hart, G, *Egyptian Myths*. British Museum Press, London, 1990.
Hornung, E, *The Valley of the Kings*. Timken, New York, 1982.
Lichteim, M, *Ancient Egyptian Literature*, 3 vols. University of California Press, Berkeley, 1980.
Lurker, M, *The Gods and Symbols of Ancient Egypt*. Thames and Hudson, London, 1980.
Nicholson, Paul and Ian Shaw, eds., *British Museum Dictionary of Ancient Egypt*. British Museum Press, London, 1995.
Pinch, G, *Magic in Ancient Egypt*. British Museum Press, London, 1994.
Quirke, S, *Ancient Egyptian Religion*. British Museum Press, London, 1959.
Reeves, N, *The Complete Tutankhamun*. Thames and Hudson, London, 1990.
Seton-Williams, M V, *Egyptian Legends and Stories*. Rubicon Press, London, 1988.
Shafer, B, ed., *Religion in Ancient Egypt*. Routledge, London, 1991.
Spence, L, *Ancient Egyptian Myths and Legends*. Dover, New York, 1990.
Spencer, A J, *Death in Ancient Egypt*. Penguin Books, Harmondsworth, 1982.
Thomas, A P, *Egyptian Gods and Myths*. Shire, Aylesbury, 1986.
Wallis Budge, E A, *The Gods of the Egyptians*. Dover, New York, 1969.
Willis, R, ed., *World Mythology*. Simon and Schuster, London, 1993.

Picture Credits